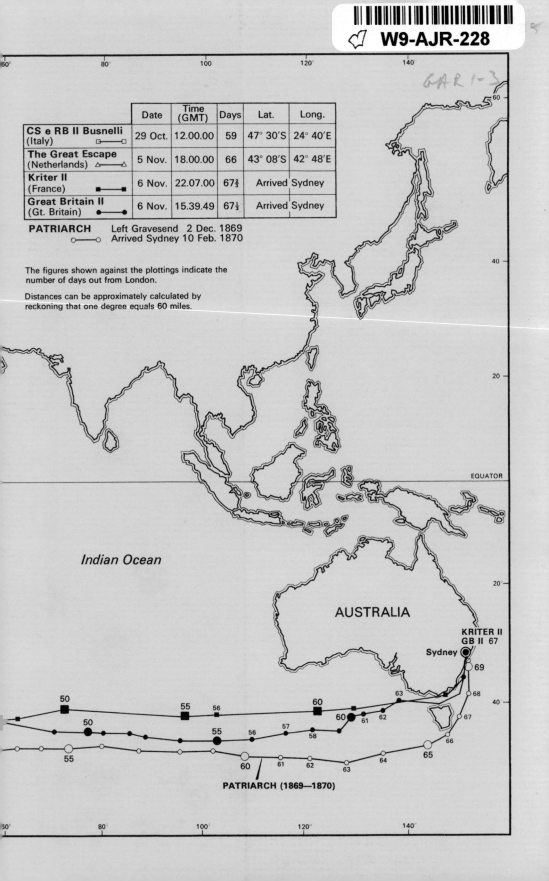

	Date	Time (GMT)	Days	Lat.	Long.
CS e RB II Busnelli (Italy) □—□	29 Oct.	12.00.00	59	47° 30′S	24° 40′E
The Great Escape (Netherlands) △—△	5 Nov.	18.00.00	66	43° 08′S	42° 48′E
Kriter II (France) ■—■	6 Nov.	22.07.00	67⅔	Arrived Sydney	
Great Britain II (Gt. Britain) ●—●	6 Nov.	15.39.49	67½	Arrived Sydney	

PATRIARCH　　Left Gravesend　2 Dec. 1869
○—○　　Arrived Sydney 10 Feb. 1870

The figures shown against the plottings indicate the
number of days out from London.

Distances can be approximately calculated by
reckoning that one degree equals 60 miles.

Indian Ocean

AUSTRALIA

KRITER II
GB II 67
Sydney

PATRIARCH (1869—1870)

Allen Lane

Alec Beilby

To Beat the Clippers

The Financial Times Clipper Race 1975-6

Allen Lane
Penguin Books Ltd,
17 Grosvenor Gardens, London SW I W OBD

First published 1976

Copyright © Alec Beilby, 1976

ISBN 0 7139 0967 6

Filmset in 'Monophoto' Ehrhardt 10 on 13 pt by
Richard Clay (The Chaucer Press) Ltd, Bungay, Suffolk
and printed in Great Britain by
Fletcher & Son Ltd, Norwich

To all those who sailed aboard *Great Britain II*, *Kriter II*, *The Great Escape*, *CS e RB II* and *Anaconda II* on their voyages from England to Australia and Australia to England, and to Captain Pile and the crew of *Patriarch* who set them a remarkable target to beat.

Contents

Race Acknowledgements

The Royal Ocean Racing Club undertook overall responsibility and the technical supervision of the race.

The following organizations gave advice and assistance, but not mentioned are the many individuals who gave generously of their time and expert help:

The Agent-General of New South Wales in London

The Australian High Commission in London

The British Antarctic Survey

The British Army

The United Kingdom High Commission in Canberra

The Commonwealth Bureau of Meteorology, Canberra

The Cruising Yacht Club of Australia

H.M. Customs and Excise

Department of Customs, Sydney

The Dover Harbour Board

The Embassies in London of The Argentine, Brazil, Chile, France, Portugal, South Africa, Spain, U.S.A., U.S.S.R.

The Good Neighbour Council of Sydney

George Hammonds (Shipping) Ltd, Dover

H.M. Department of Immigration

Department of Immigration, Sydney

St Katherine's Yacht Haven, London

Lloyds Shipping Intelligence

The Maritime Services Board, Sydney

The Ministry of Culture, Sport and Recreation in New South Wales

The Ministry of Defence, London

The Ministry of Lands in New South Wales

The New Zealand High Commission in London

Overseas Telecommunications Commission, Australia

The Port of London Authority

Post Office Telecommunications, U.K.

Qantas Airways Ltd

The Royal Air Force

The Royal Australian Navy

The Royal Australian Naval Sailing Association

The Royal Cinque Ports Yacht Club

Royal National Lifeboat Institution

The Royal Navy

The Royal Naval Sailing Association

Trinity House

The British Antarctic Survey

Although, regrettably, it has not been possible to make individual mention of the many people who gave of their time to the administration and organization of the Clipper Race, the *Financial Times* and the Race Committee would like to offer special thanks to Alan Green of the R.O.R.C., Kenneth Keenan of Qantas Airways, and Captain Jeff Gledhill, D.S.C., R.A.N. (Retd) whose special effort and help, far in excess of that asked of them, contributed so much to the success of the venture.

Race Committees

Organization of the race was in the hands of the following committees:

Race Committee formed by the Royal Ocean Racing Club

John Roome, Commodore R.O.R.C. (Chairman)
A. Churchill
Richard Davidson
The Hon. John Geddes
Col. R. H. Gilbertson, F.I.E.E.
Alan Green
Dr Nicholas Greville
Capt. J. A. Hans Hamilton, R.N. (Retd)
W. R. Matthews
Roy Mullender
Lt. Col. J. E. Myatt, R.H.A.
Alan H. Paul, O.B.E.
André Viant

Communications Sub-committee

Col. R. H. Gilbertson, F.I.E.E.
Cdr J. P. G. Gryans, R.N.
A. Churchill
A. Green

Joint Committee of the Royal Australian Naval Sailing Association and the Cruising Yacht Club of Australia

Capt. J. A. Gledhill, D.S.C., R.A.N. (Retd) (Chairman)
Capt. L. M. Hinchliffe, D.S.C., R.A.N. (Retd)
Graham Evans
Lt. Cdr W. O. C. Roberts, D.S.C., R.A.N.
Lt. Cdr P. W. Pedersen, V.R.D., R.A.N.R.
Lt. Cdr B. H. Dick, V.R.D., R.A.N.R.
K. Lawson
D. Morgan
Major L. B. Peek

List of Plates

The colour plates are reproduced by permission of the following: *Anaconda II* project, 7; *Financial Times*, 12; *Great Britain II* project, 8; *Great Britain II* project/Ian Kirkwood, 2, 3; *Great Britain II* project/David Leslie, 4, 5, 6, 9, 10, 11; Ambrose Greenway, 1.

The black-and-white plates are reproduced by permission of the following: Adelaide *Advertiser*, 48; *Anaconda II* project, 49, 65, 66; Michel Etevenson, *Kriter II* sponsor, 58, 59; *Financial Times*, 2, 12, 13, 15, 17, 18, 19, 22, 23, 24, 25, 26, 27, 28, 69, 70, 71, 72; *Financial Times*/Ministry of Defence, 30, 31; *Great Britain II* project, 32, 36, 47, 55, 56, 57; *Great Britain II* project/Ian Kirkwood, 33, 34, 35, 37, 38, 39, 40, 41, 43, 45, 46, 64; *Great Britain II* project/David Leslie, 61, 62, 63, 67, 68; Ambrose Greenway, 16, 20, 21; *Kriter II* sponsors, 29; Ministry of Defence, 10, 30, 73, 74; National Library of Australia, 4, 5, 7, 8, 9; National Maritime Museum, Greenwich, 1, 3, 6; Royal Australian Navy, 42, 44; Bob Stimson, 50, 51, 52, 53, 55.

Foreword

The Clipper Race round the world caught the imagination of sailors everywhere. The idea that modern ocean racing boats with full crews should race to Sydney and then back to Britain, a total of twenty-seven thousand miles, in an attempt to beat the record of sixty-nine days on each leg set by the clipper ship *Patriarch* in 1869–70 was indeed a challenge to the present generation both of sailors and of boatbuilders.

That *Great Britain II* succeeded not only in winning the race but also in beating that century-old record is an outstanding achievement of which we in Britain can be rightly proud. Her two crews from the Services deserve the highest praise. None the less admirable is the persistence and determination with which the French crew of *Kriter II* completed the second leg of the race after having to put back to Sydney for a refit following the loss off New Zealand of her rudder.

The four boats I started off Southend on a grey misty morning on the last day of August 1975 all completed the race, together with *Anaconda II* and her Australian crew which joined the contest at Sydney. None have received the public recognition due to them for their strenuous feats of skill and endurance.

The event was closely followed by Alec Beilby, the *Financial Times* yachting correspondent, one of our ablest and best informed sailing journalists. It is good that he has now written the whole story. This will not only give satisfaction to the crews of the competing boats and their fellow sailors; it will be of interest to a much wider public; and it will enable all of us to pay tribute to those who by their sustained efforts and personal courage created one more legend of the sea.

I was proud to start the race. I was proud to steer the victorious *Great Britain II* up the Thames into the Pool of London when it was over. I am proud to write the foreword to this record of a remarkable race.

Edward Heath

Author's Introduction

It has been argued that the best books describing events of great significance are written by those who took part. It has been argued with equal sincerity that an observer of the overall event gains a wider view than participants. It is certain that those of us able to observe the daily progress of the yachts racing in the *Financial Times* Clipper Race and who were fortunate to meet and find many helpful friends among the crew felt at times that we had been there with them on the voyage. Those at sea often had less idea of the situation aboard their rivals' yachts than those ashore in Europe and Australia but once ashore and able to compare experiences found that the problems faced and overcome aboard each yacht bore a striking similarity.

My hope is that this book has adequately described the experiences, either general or individual, of those that sailed from England to Australia and back in 1975–6 and my thanks go to all of them for help in ensuring that the words resemble the facts.

1 Early Days

In the early sixties the number of people who had sailed alone around the world, either with minimum stops or by way of a five-year cruise, could be counted on the fingers of both hands. Many of them, Joshua Slocum perhaps the most famous, had earned something of a reputation as explorers, escapists or people verging on lunacy. At about the same time the sport of single-handed offshore racing was just beginning; it was only a matter of forty years since the Royal Ocean Racing Club had been formed for those who regarded racing around predestined marks, within sight of land, as rather dull.

Among the pioneers of longer offshore racing, outside the confines of coastal waters, was Francis Chichester who, with Colonel Blondie Hasler and two others, raced single-handed in 1960 across the Atlantic from Plymouth to the Ambrose lightship off New York. Chichester won the race in forty days for half a crown ($12\frac{1}{2}$p) from Hasler plus a further £1,000 offered as prize money. He sold the exclusive story of the voyage to the *Observer*.

A new breed of yachtsmen had been born, but the cynics were quick to point to the possibility that they were, for the main part, eccentrics or old men with little to lose. Four years later the cynics were proved wrong and fifteen remarkably sane and ordinary men, Chichester among them, sailed over the course again and Eric Tabarly of France won the prize for reaching America first.

Entries for successive races continued almost to double as the races, sailed every four years, became an accepted part of the yachting fixture list. But it was in 1966–7 that Francis Chichester lifted long-distance offshore sailing into a new league.

He sailed from Plymouth in August 1966 on the specially designed and built *Gipsy Moth IV* and reached Sydney, Australia, 105 days 20 hours later. It was a remarkable voyage for any man of 65, but Chichester had already been virtually abandoned as a terminal medical case by eminent physicians six years earlier. Books by the yachtsman himself, and by others, have been written about the achievement. Chichester's return to Plymouth was watched by a crowd half a million strong. Subsequently another huge crowd watched the Queen bestow a knighthood on him at Greenwich using the sword that Queen Elizabeth I had used to knight Sir Francis Drake.

A fire had been lit and in the following seven years it was to be fanned into a furnace.

Alec Rose followed Chichester with the little yacht *Lively Lady*, and in 1968 the *Sunday Times* announced a prize of £5,000 for the winner of a race around the world from a British port and back without stopping. This race, through no real fault of the organizers, almost became a complete tragedy. The Frenchman Bernard Moitissier sailed around the world aboard *Joshua*, passing the Capes of Good Hope and Horn and then, instead of heading north for certain victory, continued on past the Cape of Good Hope and Australia a second time, eventually stopping on a French Pacific island. Nigel Tetley lost his yacht trying to beat the mysterious Donald Crowhurst who had sailed his trimaran in circles in the southern Atlantic rather than give up or face the perils of the Southern Ocean. Tetley had sailed the full distance around the world never doubting that Crowhurst had done the same thing but unaware of the other yachtsman's position. Once into the southern fringe of the North Atlantic ocean Tetley began to receive reports indicating that Crowhurst was astern of him but making up ground fast so, although his trimaran *Victress* was a little strained, Tetley crammed on maximum sail in rough to fresh conditions resulting in severe strain and the eventual sinking of his yacht. Luckily he was able to send an emergency message and was found by the U.S. Coastguard patrol aircraft after only two days at sea in his liferaft.

Books have been written about this race too. It was won by the redoubtable Robin Knox-Johnston with his little ketch *Suhaili*, the only entrant to complete the course. It was a field day for the critics of this sort of sailing but fortunately Knox-Johnston was strong enough and sane enough at the end of the voyage to prove that his motives for competing were completely reasonable.

The seeds for a race for fully crewed yachts around the world were now sown. In 1971 Anthony Churchill, already established as one of the best navigators in offshore racing, joined forces with Guy Pearse, a professional promoter, to organize a race planned to start in 1973. They sought interest in the yachting empire and sponsors from without, but while yachtsmen were cautiously interested, sponsors were harder to woo. The Navy had a new Camper & Nicholson 55-footer on the stocks and were enthusiastic about a race of this length, so the Royal Naval Sailing Association took over the promotion of the race and persuaded Whitbread, the London-based brewers, to help with sponsorship. Once the race seemed to be on rather than just a possibility, interest increased among yachtsmen throughout the world.

2 The Whitbread–R.N.S.A. Race

In 1972 yachtsmen and famous designers could be seen deep in conference in the various centres in London and farther afield. The indomitable Chay Blyth, who achieved perhaps the ultimate voyage by sailing *British Steel* single-handed non-stop around the world against the prevailing winds and currents, was seen in just such a conference with Alan Gurney, a British designer who worked from New York and had a number of successful large offshore racing yachts, including *Windward Passage*, to his credit. The Naval yacht, to be named *Adventure*, was almost complete and other famous names of the deepwater racing game were busy, Eric Tabarly, Doi Malingri di Bagnolo and Eric Pascoli among them.

It seemed, as the spring of 1973 passed, that there might be twenty starters from Portsmouth on the first stage of the race to Cape Town, South Africa, but when the vast ancient cannon boomed across the waters of Spithead sixteen yachts set out, surrounded and at times almost thwarted by the largest armada of small craft ever seen. It even exceeded that famous fleet that accompanies the start of the annual race from Sydney to Hobart, which the Australians found hard to believe.

About this time, several weeks before the start of the Whitbread– R.N.S.A. race the curtain was raised on a plan for a further race around the world, with only one stop in Sydney, in 1975. I was probably as surprised as many others, for it had been a well-kept secret and, again, was the brainchild of Anthony Churchill and Guy Pearse. Yachtsmen and yachting journalists alike were immersed in the Admiral's Cup and then the Whitbread–R.N.S.A. race. In the middle of this excitement I was summoned to the offices of the *Financial Times* to talk about 'the race around the world'. Assuming that this was the race which was about to start, I travelled to London, where John Geddes, head of the promotions department at the *Financial Times*, unveiled the plans for the *Financial Times* Clipper Race, to be sailed around the world in 1975 from the estuary of the Thames to Sydney and back to Dover. The objective of the race was to beat the fastest run made by a Clipper ship of the last century with maximum-sized modern yachts racing without the International Offshore Rule handicap system.

The idea seemed as adventurous as it was novel. Reaction even among those already committed to the 1973 race was enthusiastic, although, naturally enough, their immediate sights were set no further ahead than Cape Town, Sydney, Rio de Janeiro and Portsmouth. Even before that race began, notice was being taken by the Clipper Race promoters of the safety requirements, the demands on yachts and crews and the communications problems that had to be faced and solved by the Whitbread organizers and competitors. This was not poaching but learning. Safety regulations based on decisions already made for the Whitbread race were provisionally incorporated in the Clipper Race rules and early advice to intending competitors. Standards carefully drawn up by the organizers for the first race were similarly included in the compulsory requirements for the Clipper Race; advisers for one race in several instances became advisers for the second.

In time, all sailors will benefit from these long-distance races. As with motor-racing, offshore racing provides a test-bed for ideas and equipment that eventually find their way – in a cheaper form – aboard the more humble cruising boat.

The paths of the two races crossed several times even before the 1973 race had started. A deputation from the *Financial Times* and the Royal Ocean Racing Club, the club that was to organize and supervise the Clipper Race, travelled to Australia in the summer of 1973 to sound out local feeling, opinion and enthusiasm for the event. Certainly the reception was favourable. Unfortunately the wires became somewhat crossed at this point. Preparations for the arrival of the yachts in the 1973 Whitbread race had received, at this stage, little publicity in Sydney, for this was being handled by the Royal Australian Navy and the Royal Australian Naval Sailing Association. When the tired, exhilarated sailors reached Sydney in December 1973 the Australians were thinking in terms of the Clipper Race, and it was some time before the fact dawned that there were to be two races within two years from Europe to Australia. Once the enthusiasm and confusion had been unravelled, the delight of Australian yachtsmen and those that live near the sea in that great country was unbounded.

The Whitbread race yachts reached Sydney to find a continual round of receptions, parties and less formal gatherings that culminated with Christmas in Sydney before their restart three days later for Cape Horn and Rio de Janeiro. Their visit was marred only by the loss of two lives during the stage from Cape Town to Sydney, but neither was lost because the yachts were racing around the world. The accidents that caused both losses were not more nor less likely to be met with during an ocean race in the English Channel in severe weather. Recovering those overboard was trickier merely because a yacht is very much on its own in the wastes of the Southern Ocean. One thing that did emerge from these tragedies was that safety harnesses and equipment were vital to survival and that minimum standards for equipment needed investigation.

One of those who observed the arrival of the 1973 race in Sydney was the Australian yachtsman Josko Grubic, owner then of the attractive cruiser-er–racer *Anaconda*, who was in Sydney to take part in the ocean race from Sydney to Hobart, Tasmania. A cheerful extrovert, he was already planning his yacht for the Clipper Race as he sailed for Tasmania while a syndicate in New Zealand were also showing interest.

Back in London the provisional race committee included Captain Hans Hamilton, also on the committee of the Whitbread Race, John Roome of the Royal Ocean Racing Club, and Anthony Churchill. Meanwhile discussions were taking place in other quarters as it was realized that the Clipper Race fortunately coincided with various other celebrations.

In 1975 fell the fiftieth anniversary of the Royal Ocean Club and of the Royal Yachting Association. The R.Y.A. is the national British authority that coordinates both competitive and non-competitive sailing in the British Isles. It was also the two hundredth anniversary of the founding of one of the oldest yacht clubs in the world, the Royal Thames, based in Knightsbridge and called in its early days the Duke of Cumberland's fleet. All these bodies might come together for some form of celebration before the start of the Clipper Race at the end of August; it was hoped that the gathering could be put to some profitable use to help a cause that was associated with yachting, the Organization of Sail Training Associations, and with a feel for the clipper ships of the past.

After deliberation with the Royal Yachting Association and others it was decided that the Organization of Sea Training Associations would be the main beneficiary. This organization is the international controlling body of all sail training associations including Britain's.

The original idea was to hold a regatta in the Thames for training ships and yachtsmen from Britain and the European ports bordering the

North Sea and the English Channel. A second committee was established with representatives from the Sail Training Association, the London Division of the Royal Naval Volunteer Reserve, the City of London and other bodies that might wish to be involved or which might become involved whether or not they had intended to be. It could be said that the Greater London Council and the Inner London Education Authority were among the latter, although once involved their help was invaluable.

Like a small snowball rolling down hill, the planned regatta became increasingly bigger until even those who had followed the scheme since the first meetings, could not quite believe the obvious success of the venture.

The planning of both the Clipper Race itself and the Festival of Sail which preceded it involved many people from a wide range of official bodies as well as many individuals who simply wanted to become part of the overall pattern. There was plenty of work to be handled, and it was Tony Bell, secretary and overall coordinator of Festival of Sail, who kept up the initial momentum and, at the same time, held costs within the prescribed budget and reality.

By happy coincidence, and coincidence had a great deal to do with the smooth running and success of the Festival, it had long been planned to hold a rally of training ships and yachts at Amsterdam during the week preceding the Festival. It almost guaranteed that careful persuasion would ensure that some, if not all, of those sailing to Holland could be persuaded to call at London before dispersing. The Port of London Authority, which in recent years had taken more and more interest in the use of their waters for leisure following the decline of merchant trade in the Thames, was pleased to help. They had already promoted the Festival during the International Boat Show, in London, and proposed special moorings for the expected square-rigged ships and for the hundreds of yachtsmen who planned to visit the Pool of London for the occasion.

The full support of the Port of London Authority was the vital ingredient for the success of the Festival and Commander Paul Satow stepped well beyond the bounds that might have been expected to restrict him to ensure that there was a place for every ship, launches available to ferry those ashore who were moored in the river and help available of every imaginable sort.

Meetings between the Festival organizers, the Sail Training Association and other organizations involved took on a new dimension when the scope of the Port of London Authority's plans became evident, much of this discussion taking place a year before the opening date of the Festival. This enabled the managing committee of the Festival to send definite assurances to the masters and managers of the world's largest training ships that their appearance in London would not only be welcomed but professionally handled and since the schedules of these ships are often decided years ahead this in itself was a prime factor in persuading them to bring their ships either from the Amsterdam rally or, in some cases, from further afield.

As the Whitbread race was drawing to its end at Portsmouth news was reaching London from Australia of a second entry from 'down under', a rival to Josko Grubic's *Anaconda II*. Jack Rooklyn, then the owner of the sloop *Apollo I* that Alan Bond had built as a training yacht for his 12-metre American Cup crew, was reported to be holding discussions with Australian yacht designer Bob Miller. A maximum-sized International Offshore Rule sloop, built in aluminium and measuring 72 foot on the waterline, was said to be in mind. While the hope of these two entries from Australia added spice to the potential of the race other inquiries arrived from Holland, Poland, Russia and the United States.

A ferro-concrete yacht was known to be under construction on an island on the river Seine a few miles from Paris and a crew of disabled ex-servicemen were holding trials on the north coast of France aboard the ketch *Veline*, a sistership to Bernard Moitissier's *Joshua*.

It seemed that as soon as one potential entry was announced others decided that it was time to declare their intentions, and a team of yachtsmen from the Joint Services Sailing Association then announced that they were to charter Chay Blyth's *Great Britain II* and sail the race with a change of crews at Sydney.

Selection of the Service crews began in the autumn of 1974 and it was planned to take over the yacht for special refitting and final crew selection during the early spring of 1975. As in the Whitbread race the Services entry declared their ambition of taking part before anyone else. While crews were planning, other individual yachtsmen were offering their services for the race, with skills ranging from a German master mariner with experience in the square-rigged German training ship to two state-registered nurses.

8

1. *Patriarch* lying at anchor, laden, in the lower reaches of the Thames. A Thames sailing barge can be seen in the background, right

2. The *Patriarch* Trophy. Comparison of the $\frac{1}{8}$ inch to the foot model with the *Patriarch* herself shows the accuracy of her building by Basset-Lowke of Northampton. The rigging alone required 200 feet of silk cord

Should there have been a yacht owner without a crew Roddie Ainslie, who had skippered the 71-foot ketch *Second Life* in the Whitbread race, offered himself and almost his entire crew for the Clipper Race. Sadly this offer was never taken up though Bill King-Harman, who sailed the Sydney to Rio de Janeiro leg of the Whitbread aboard *Second Life*, was eventually selected for the Sydney to Dover stage of the Clipper Race as a watch leader aboard *Great Britain II*.

The Racing Secretary of the Royal Ocean Racing Club, Alan Green, and Roy Mullender, who had skippered the Naval yacht *Adventure* on the final leg of the Whitbread Race and after sailing the third stage from Australia to Rio as one of her crew, compiled special safety regulations based on experiences gathered over nearly fifty years of offshore racing and especially during the Whitbread Race. The resulting work is one of the most comprehensive documents on safety at sea for small craft and proves again that from long races around the world comes experience to help even the humblest family sailor whose voyaging may never go beyond the local bay. It is reproduced in Appendix 1, pages 163–78. The hunt into the records of the ships sailing between Britain and Australia was wide and various. Experts investigated archives both in London and Australia. The famous clipper *Thermopylae* was at one time in the running and it was already known that *Cutty Sark* had made the voyage in about a hundred days in each direction, but it was from London to Sydney, not Melbourne, that needed the greatest research and it was in Sydney rather than London that the story of the remarkable voyage of the Aberdeen-registered ship *Patriarch* was uncovered, together with photographs of some of her crew and passengers who had shipped aboard for her record-breaking run from London to Sydney, sixty-nine days, in 1869.

Whether or not *Patriarch* was the holder of the record run from Britain to Australia or, indeed, from Sydney back to Britain was still a mystery. Basil Bathe, the assistant keeper in charge of the Water Transport Collections at the Science Museum, London, was asked for his opinion as was another much respected maritime historian David Macgregor. David Macgregor had recently written a book, *Fast Sailing Ships, 1775–1875*, which mentioned *Patriarch*, but only in the context as to whether the ship qualified for the title of clipper. He conceded that she did, but no mention was made of her remarkable voyage.

At a luncheon held at the *Financial Times*, attended by both these emin-ent historians and others whose knowledge of the old ships must have made the occasion unique, it was agreed that *Patriarch* was the holder of the record and model-makers were commissioned to build an exact scale replica of the ship as the principal prize for the race. This in itself was a difficult task because no docking plans, line drawings or other details apart from old photographs were available to the modellers but the eventual result was a credit to their skills and graced the windows of the *Financial Times* building in Cannon Street for some weeks before the race began.

3 Patriarch

Patriarch, then, was the record-holding ship, although she had never earned the reputation that remains to this day of the *Cutty Sark*. Research produced a number of details about her that deserve mention here.

The ship, owned by the Aberdeen Line and built by Walter Hood of Aberdeen, was launched in 1869 for a cost of £24,000. She was constructed of iron and had a gross tonnage of a little under 1,500 tons. She was three-masted and was relatively unusual in having top gallant masts of telescopic construction, so they could be lowered in severe weather inside the main body of the masts below. This was not a new idea, but a conception of the 1850s, and with steel rigging it is unlikely that the mast ever needed to be lowered in this way. Yet it is worth noting that *Patriarch*, unlike some of her contemporaries, was never dismasted and in 1892 she survived a cyclone in the Indian Ocean which almost overwhelmed a larger ship only seventy miles away.

Her first master, Captain Pile, took her from the stocks in her builders' yard and, reaching London in the early autumn of 1869, sailed for Australia as winter began to set in. Her voyage to Australia was reported in the Sydney *Morning Herald* in late February 1870 and enjoyed by Australian settlers who were happy to be able to read London news and newspapers that had been published only a little more than two months earlier.

The *Patriarch*'s record-breaking voyage was recorded by a passenger in the article which follows. It gives a clear insight to the weather conditions that can be expected on a voyage of this sort as well as an idea of life aboard one of the fastest ships of the age:

The newspapers by this mail will tell you of our arrival here on the 10th instant after making the most rapid passage on record, being only sixty-nine days from Gravesend. There was considerable excitement about the event all over the town, and the honor of it, of course exclusively due to the ship and its commander, seemed to be extended to the passengers and crew as well. At all events, one had

3. *Patriarch* in dry dock, probably in Australia during the
late nineteenth century. Note the fine entry of her bow

4. *Patriarch* in her later years, under sail off the Australian coast

occasionally to submit to half sceptical questioning as to the weather, distances, to the Line, to the Cape, as to our southing and the like. To some who were envious of our success, and who would state in a matter of course way, 'Oh, you have had remarkable luck in weather,' it was specially pleasant, as well as quite truthful, to say in reply 'Oh, by no means, we had little favour in the weather, beyond others. We had light winds, variable winds, and no winds at all when we ought to have had the "trades"; and if we had had merely average luck at certain stages of our course, we might have made it in ten days less easily.'

A very common plan of reckoning by which to the uninitiated the time is shortened, and the vessel's credit is enhanced or lessened, as the case may be, is to cut off both the day of start from the land and of arrival, on the plea of both being broken days; and there may be many days spent in the Downs waiting a favourable start, and no account taken of them in announcing the duration of the voyage, although the anxious passengers count every one, whether included in the run or not. Our time, as you will observe, being from Gravesend, is to be considered as something very wonderful indeed.

A voyage from England to New South Wales is not an everyday affair, and it is only a few comparatively that have opportunity or occasion to undertake it. But on the whole, when once the preliminary disagreeables of the very moving incidents of the flood are over, as also the novelty of being cribbed, cabined or confined, and when you have come to regard your surroundings with a precision of knowledge and familiarity of old acquaintance, there is little else to be experienced. That long voyages, except in rare instances, are as much alike as possible every one knows. There is the usual chorus of the sailors at their work, whether at the ropes, pumps or deck holystoning, and the usual variables of the weather. The routine goes on ceaselessly, with the half-hour striking of the watch bell on the poop, and the responsive echo from the forecastle, and these monotonous but simultaneous, and prolonged ringing of the stewards bell for meals.

After meals, the smokers usually compare meerschaums and do a little additional colouring work; then the walk up and down the deck, or the novels or game of some sort. Such was the progress initiated with weighing anchor in the stream at Gravesend, and faithfully adhered to all these sixty-nine days, from the casting off respectively of the tug-steamer and the river and Channel pilots, and on through the trough-like sea of the Bay of Biscay and Atlantic; the calms, sudden squalls, and streaming rains of the tropics, to the long rollers of the Pacific; and finally to our journey's end between the heads of Sydney harbour. In the Channel we dipped our colours to an American iron-clad steaming on to join the convoy of honour to the remains of Mr Peabody; and abreast of Cape Finnisterre, going more than twelve knots under a cloud of canvas, we ran up our number to a Norwegian or Danish Barque under close-reefed topsails homeward bound and who, we were afterwards glad to learn, had reported us correctly. Other vessels were sighted occasionally, and the few going our course we duly overhauled and dropped astern without loss of time. But for many days there was nothing to note. Madeira, forty-five miles off, we did not see, and going outside of Cape Verde Islands, the small Trinidad, south of the Line, was the first land seen, and, afterwards, the Islands of Tristan D'Achunha, both presenting much the same aspect of high and desolate-looking rocks.

The ceremony of the crossing of the Line was duly attended to, but on the same evening, while in continuance of the amusements, most of the passengers and crew had assembled on the main deck doing some singing and recitations, the cry, 'Man overboard,' startled every one, and changed in a moment the pleasant aspect of affairs. All rushed out, and both lifebuoys were thrown out almost at a venture, as it was now dark and the ship going well through the water. Immediately the excited but prompt and brief words of command from the cabin got every one of the crew to work; and while breathless questions – 'Who is it? Who is it?' – were asked on every side, the ship was put aback with the greatest promptitude, and the lifeboat lowered for the search. Not very many but very anxious were the moments, but relief came when the cheer from the crew of the lifeboat was heard, and shortly they emerged from the darkness, and they and their dripping messmate stepped on deck safe and sound. The boat was slung again to the davits, and we proceeded on our course as before.

As usual, the pretty little Mother Carey's Chickens were the first to make their appearance in our wake, and to bear them ceremony came the mollymank, the black frigate-bird, the beautifully marked Cape pigeon, and the enormous albatross – these last sometimes in great numbers, not one of which, however, would take the bait of fat pork seductively thrown out with a long line from the poop.

Also, the flying fish flitting like so many swallows – only one lighting on board was caught; the dolphin and porpoise racing alongside and across our path, out of one wave through space into the breast of another; and last and greatest, a monster whale heaving up his black shoulders and spouting at intervals.

The cold of Gravesend, where the water buckets had frozen fast, rapidly gave way to the mildness of Madeira, and the temperature increased till the thermometer stood at 82 degrees in the shade in the tropics, and then again diminished till, when at 51 degrees south latitude, light clothing had long

5. The upper deck of *Patriarch*. On her best run in the
Southern Ocean during her record-breaking run to Sydney,
Patriarch covered 370 miles in a day, averaging 15 knots

6. Games aboard *Patriarch* at sea: the second mate wins
the hand-over-hand competition

7. A rare interior picture of the main officers' and passengers' dining saloon, the table laid for Christmas dinner at sea

8. Loading the final bales of wool aboard *Patriarch*, using a screw-jack (seen in the top corner of the hatch), to compress the wool and avoid air being trapped and causing a severe fire risk

9. *Patriarch* unloading cargo in Sydney in the 1890s. Although she was more than thirty years old, her owners, the Aberdeen Line, maintained her appearance to their customary high standards

disappeared, and unmitigated idleness beneath the shelter of the awning gave place to violent exercise, vigorous attempts at keeping up the circulation, and disputes as to the best cure for chilblains. Going so far south as we did, on the great circle sailing principle, we had nice short degrees of easting to do, and we polished them off at the average rate of seven a day, each of these days, of course, being shortened by nearly half an hour; in two days of something less than twenty-three and a half hours we made 670 miles.

Northward bound at last, towards the corner of Tasmania, but passing too far off to see it, we left behind the vigorous breezes of the South Pacific, which had answered the purpose of our southing so well; and with a light wind, and for the most part dead aft, we continued due north, till at noon on 9th instant, following a night of incessant rolling, caused by the swell and lightness of the wind, we caught sight of the Australian coast. At this time the weather was hazy, and we were still a long way off, and an hour or two elapsed till the land, which lay like a light cloud along the horizon, assumed the consistency of a bold coastline, with some mountains in the distant interior, the loftiest probably Mount Dromedary, 2600 feet above the level of the sea.

The wind freshening a little, and being off the land, we slipped along the coast at about ten knots an hour, when, during dinner, the officer of the watch announced 'land on the lea bow sir', which proved to be the looked-for St George's Head in the dim distance. Altering our course just a little, St George's Head, Jervis Bay, and Point Perpendicular were breasted early in the evening. The setting sun shed its light full on the breast of the heights, and made the sombre-tinted herbage and solitary-looking stunted trees which had their abode there look their brightest. But an almost marked sense of uninhabited vastness of these regions came upon one. No friendly feathery messengers came to greet us from the land; and the mollymanks and albatross still following in our wake paid no need to it. Silence, vastness, and gloom ruled unchallenged, save by the slanting rays of the sun, doubtless also by the roar of the shooting columns of spray along the steeps, too distant to be heard by us, but breaking with the full force of the Pacific, and plainly visible miles away, Botany Bay, the town of Ranwich on the heights – almost a suburb of Sydney – and Sydney Heads and lighthouse appeared duly next morning.

About halfpast six a.m., a steamer and pilot took us in tow, and hoisting our ensign and number, we passed between the heads of the famous Port Jackson or Sydney harbour. The scene into which we were now introduced baffles all attempts adequately to describe it. There was a singularity of character in the beauty of the apparently innumerable bays and headlands and small green-clad islands opening up to view at every instant as we quietly glided along with the aid of the steamer. The calm and shelter and warmth which we had reached had a charmingly soothing influence. The atmosphere was of Italian-like purity, and there was a freshness of colouring of a Norwegian fiord, without, of course, the grandeur and sterility of the Norwegian mountain; but instead, there were abrupt slopes on the right hand and the left, undulating and extending in variety of outline, and thickly clad to the edge of the water, with strange-looking bushes and grasses of dark green. But on all sides a most remarkable noise startled all those who, like myself, were new to the country. Myriads of locusts had taken possession, and made a sound as if a million fine-toothed circular saws were hard at work on some close-grained material. The novelty of the scene and sound was very striking, and we had scarcely patience to go below. But at anchor, at some distance from the quay, we had breakfast on an even keel once more. By and by boats came and went back, and we had news from home only one day later than we brought with us. Passengers separated to see their friends and make acquaintance with the town, and settle for lodgings and luggage – some pairing off together, others going alone, all alike to devour with varying gusto, doubtless, the ripe grapes, peaches, pine apples, and melons so much in profusion here at this season, and all alike to run the gauntlet of the daring mosquito, who never fails to court with avidity the fresh blood of the old country. And so ended our voyage.

4 The Yachts Prepare

During the winter of 1974–5 international recession and its accompanying financial problems were reaching their worst for more than thirty years, yet this was the time when those intending to participate in the Clipper Race had to commit themselves finally one way or the other. With the list of potential starters hovering around ten yachts, it seemed that many who had expressed interest earlier had already sensed the forthcoming financial climate and dropped the idea. As if to emphasize her intentions the Dutch yacht *The Great Escape* arrived in the Thames carrying a Christmas tree in her rigging, or was it the famous broom carried by the Dutch Admiral van Tromp, with which he intended to sweep the British from the oceans of the world? A steel ketch, she was owned by Watersports Twellegea, a Dutch sailing school specializing in offshore training and chartering, and would, it seemed, be one of the smaller yachts taking part.

Meanwhile the Joint Services plans for *Great Britain II* were progressing down in Plymouth, where the yacht was laid up for the winter, and at the Joint Services Sailing Centre at Gosport, Hampshire. The Italians were well ahead with their plans aboard the schooner *CS e RB II* and were intending to compete in the transatlantic race from New York to Portsmouth, a race arranged to coincide with the Royal Thames Yacht Club bi-centenary celebrations.

In Paris Serge Moreau and his team building the ferro-concrete yacht on the Seine were still optimistic that they would find financial backing.

While the French ex-servicemen were still planning in and around Cherbourg other Frenchmen were wondering how they might be able to take part and, most important as far as French patriotism was concerned, win the race. Time was already too short to build a yacht specifically for the race but there were one or two around that could certainly win given the right crew, just as there were more than enough fine French sailors available to sail such a yacht if it could be found.

Eric Tabarly's ketch *Pen Duick VI* was laid up on the west coast of

France. He had already said that he felt it unlikely that he would sail the course again so soon after the earlier race, but some, knowing how little Tabarly was inclined to give away, even to friends, still believed that he might be at the starting line. Less reticent was Michel Etevenon, the promoter of Kriter and Patriarche wines, from the Beaune region of France, who had supported the hard-sailed ketch *Kriter* which took fourth place overall in the Whitbread race. The problem was finding a yacht and early indications showed that Leslie Williams's and Alan Smith's *Burton Cutter*, preparing for charter in the Greek islands, could be available for a long charter to take part.

By the time possible terms had been negotiated between the owners, their agents and the potential charterers the yacht had sailed for the Mediterranean. Michel Etevenon, who already had his crew in mind, asked that the yacht put into the French Riviera and sent Olivier de Kersauson to hold trials and evaluate the possibilities of the yacht taking overall line honours on both legs of the Clipper Race against *Great Britain II*. While these trials were being held in the Mediterranean sad news reached London from Australia.

The building of *Anaconda II* had proceeded without problems, or no more problems than those that normally face the builders of a 'one-off' yacht of maximum size. Her launching date and trials were timed so that she could sail from Australia with special clearance from the Egyptian government to pass through the recently cleared and re-opened Suez Canal on her way to Britain. It was even hoped that she might be able to sail in the British ocean racing classic to the Fastnet Rock as part of final trails, though the voyage to Britain, with a cruising crew, would almost certainly have given her an edge over the other yachts in the Clipper Race.

During the launching ceremony Josko Grubic, her owner, fell from a scaffold and was badly injured. Clearly he would not be able to sail with the yacht to Europe and plans were then put to hand to ship the yacht aboard a freighter. Cost was a problem for a yacht is measured for shipment against the number of standard containers that she displaces and a yacht of 80 foot in length displaces a lot. Shipping dates also presented problems, and as the final deadline approached the financial and material difficulties were beginning to overshadow and outweigh the enthusiasm of the owner and crew. Even if the yacht had reached London there would have been virtually no time for testing the yacht after her rigging had been refitted and the stores for the voyage loaded so, sadly, she was withdrawn from the first leg but was to be prepared to sail from Sydney to London.

One by one the numbers began to drop but by May preceding the start it seemed increasingly apparent that Michel Etevenon had found the yacht he wanted for de Kersauson and his crew.

Burton Cutter, to be renamed *Kriter II* and to fly the French flag, sailed from southern France to Lymington and in France a complete refit of her deck layout and accommodation, apart from ambitious storage planning, was planned. Meanwhile the crew of *Veline* withdrew and the starting list from London was down to four which could be divided into two pairs, *Great Britain II* and *Kriter II* to battle for the line honours while the Italian schooner *CS e RB II* and the Dutch ketch *The Great Escape* would probably drop behind and develop their own struggle for handicap honours and line honours of their own.

5 The Yachts and Their Crews

The largest of the four yachts to be on the starting-line would be the Joint Services entry, *Great Britain II*, already a veteran from the 1973–4 race with a circumnavigation of the world of 141 days behind her and proven ability in the oceans of the world. Selection of her crew had been rigorously and carefully planned after invitations to members of all the services had been advertised.

Care was taken not to antagonize those who might have objected to thirty-two servicemen setting out on a three-month cruise at tax-payers' expense; it was pointed out, first that the exercise would be an adventure training project and secondly that it was sponsored by outside financial help and funds raised within the armed forces on a voluntary basis. Originally, the special committee organizing the project estimated that the charter fee and the cost of the project itself would total about £30,000. The problems of raising this sort of money and the uncertainty of such calculations in a time of economic recession were to change something quite feasible to a problem of nightmarish proportions.

Applications for crew positions flooded in from every corner of the globe, and from every rank of serving man. The committee sifted the names, the experience of each man and his availability and by early 1975 the nucleus of the two crews, one for each leg, had emerged for training aboard the yacht. Priority was given to the first-leg crew as it was thought possible that the second-leg crew would have ample time in Sydney between the two stages of the race to come to know their yacht well. The yacht, meanwhile, had been refitted at Mashfords shipyard, at Cremyll near Plymouth, the scene of so many famous refits in the past of both world-girdling yachts and those in the early single-handed transatlantic races.

Great Britain II, designed by Alan Gurney, was built in Kent in 1973 by Derek Kelsall of sandwich foam construction and launched prior to the Whitbread race by Princess Anne. Designed specifically for voyages of this sort, the yacht had unique features including specially strengthened rigging, accommodation for up to sixteen men working a three-watch

10.   The British ketch *Great Britain II*, during sail training
prior to the Clipper Race

11. *Burton Cutter* seen competing in the annual Round the Island race.
She was chartered for the Clipper Race by the French and renamed
Kriter II

12. The crew of *Kriter II* in London during a ceremony of blessing by the Bishop of Beaune. Her skipper Olivier de Kersauson and navigator Yves Olivaux are seen far left

13. The crew of *CS e RB II*. Far left is Geoff Cross from Lancashire. Her skipper Doi Malingri is third from the left with Elnora Waring, one of the three girls in the race

system, and sails for the tempestuous seas of the Southern Ocean, the Atlantic and the Southern Pacific. Her original maximum sail area comprised a foretriangle of 1,400 square feet, a mainsail of 862 square feet and a mizzen sail area of 276 square feet, but the foretriangle area was increased and her biggest headsail, a magnificent sight when set, was of almost 2,400 square feet in area and the largest spinnaker carried for the race was about twice as large as this.

Below decks the skipper, the radio operator and the navigator shared the aft cabin for working and sleeping while forward of the engine area the quarters for the rest of the crew were divided into three sleeping areas, a galley and a saloon. While one watch was on deck the standby watch could be available below without disturbing those off watch and sleeping. Two teams of twenty-two men were chosen from which two crews of fifteen and sixteen respectively were selected for the race.

In France selecting and training the crew of *Kriter II* was more hurried. The decision to charter and refit the yacht, still *Burton Cutter* of Whitbread race fame, was not taken until well into the spring of 1975. While she was sailed back from the Mediterranean to Lymington for a complete refit at the Berthon shipyard her skipper, Olivier de Kersauson, began selecting his final team. There was plenty of potential in France to choose from, but availability at such short notice for a voyage of six months or more was another matter. De Kersauson had crewed on various yachts from Tabarly's *Pen Duick* stable; he looked both at his former fellows and at men who had crewed the earlier *Kriter* for his team.

His choice was interesting and in some ways predictable. Georges Commarmond, cook and bosun of *Kriter I* joined with Patrick Meulemeester, a former first-leg crewman aboard *Pen Duick VI*, and a selection of other predominantly younger yachtsmen. The oldest member of the crew was the veteran Air France captain, 65-year-old Yves Olivaux, as navigator; he had sailed the last leg of the 1973 race aboard Eric Pascoli's yacht *Taranga*. In all they were a formidable crew with the right balance of age, youth and experience led by an experienced man with an open cheerful attitude to life that made him a fine leader for his crew.

Crew training aboard *Kriter II* was absolutely minimal before the start because the alterations, refitting and final rebuilding of the accommodation below deck after extensive hull strengthening left little time for

31

14.   The Italian schooner *CS e RB II* under sail during trials

15.   The smallest yacht to sail in the Clipper Race, the
Dutch ketch *The Great Escape*, heading down the Thames
for the start of the race

THE GREAT ESCAPE

Clipper Race

anything else. The complete working deck forward of the cockpit was removed and replaced at Lymington, the replacement looking as though it had been taken from *Pen Duick VI* and covered with the heavy self-tailing winches so dear to French hearts.

Below decks the accommodation was drastically altered, partly because of the alterations above decks and partly to prepare the yacht for the voyage ahead, for she had earlier been refitted by her owners, Leslie Williams and Alan Smith, for charter in the Adriatic and Mediterranean. The bow frames and stringers in the aluminium hull, which had cracked during the Whitbread race and led to the yacht's retirement off South Africa, had again been doubled by the French. As *Burton Cutter* the yacht had led the way to Cape Town so de Kersauson and his crew knew that they had a fast and capable yacht, but when they reached London for the final week of preparation the experience of the crew at actually sailing their craft was limited and the scene below decks was chaotic.

This was not the case with Doi Malingri and his team aboard the Italian yacht *CS e RB II*. Malingri, skipper of the first curiously named *CS e RB* in the Whitbread race and a veteran of Cape Horn and single-handed transatlantic yacht racing, had chosen his yacht for the Clipper Race carefully. The new yacht was a sister ship to the French schooner *Grand Louis* which André Viant and his family, plus a few friends, had sailed, apparently so easily and successfully, in the Whitbread race. She was delivered to Malingri well ahead of schedule, so he had, as planned, taken the yacht and her crew for the race across the Atlantic to America and then sailed back from Newport to Portsmouth in the race organized as part of the bicentenary celebrations of the Royal Thames and New York Yacht Clubs.

Among his crew of seven he chose an Englishman, Geoff Cross, from Lytham St Annes, who was to become one of the more colourful characters of the race, and fashion model Elnora Waring whose knowledge of yoga and vegetarian cooking was initially to raise eyebrows but later to prove useful. On arrival in the Thames for the start Doi Malingri probably had the most experienced crew of the four in knowing the workings and foibles of their craft.

Finally the smallest yacht in the race, the Dutch ketch *The Great Escape*, was obviously not the fastest in the fleet but seemed the most comfortable. Built of steel and with a very practical if heavy rig, the yacht, below

34

decks, was reminiscent of a Dutch coaster, providing adequate if some-what cramped accommodation for her skipper, Henk Huisman, and his crew of twelve, all paying members of the sailing school who owned her; some of the crew, including the skipper, were to change in Sydney. When she arrived in London, escorted by other yachts of the same breed from the sailing-school fleet, her deckhouse, high stern and square yards seemed more suitable for an extended cruise of the Caribbean rather than a chase to Australia where handicap was of secondary importance and the Southern Ocean and the Roaring Forties the biggest hurdles in the obstacle race.

Unlike the Whitbread–R.N.S.A. race, the Clipper Race was not primarily to be decided on the International Offshore Rule of handicap. It had been apparent during the earlier race, both to the crews and those who followed the race, that the greatest kudos went to the first boat home. Certainly the handicap system added further interest but, for example, the arrival of *Pen Duick VI* at the Sydney finishing line less than ten hours ahead of *Great Britain II* after a voyage of more than 6,000 miles was remarkable and exciting. The I.O.R. formula of handicap, based on the yachts' measurements, produces a 'time correction factor' (T.C.F.). The actual time taken over the course is multiplied by the yacht's T.C.F. to give a time corrected for handicap. Suppose a yacht with a T.C.F. of 1.000 takes 36 hours for a race; her corrected time is $36 \times 1.000 = 36$. A much smaller yacht with a T.C.F. of 0.500 might take twice as long – 72 hours – for the same course; her corrected time is $72 \times 0.500 = 36$, so the two yachts finish equal on handicap. The calcula-tion is never quite as cut and dried as that and very few results end identically but the system does mean that, theoretically, large and small yachts compete on a common basis.

The *Financial Times* Clipper Race was planned as an exercise in which modern yachts, limited to the maximum size acceptable under the International Offshore Rule, would attempt to beat one another on a boat-for-boat basis and, at the same time, beat *Patriarch*'s times. The Royal Ocean Racing Club, as guardians of the handicap system, offered two clocks as prizes for the best corrected, or handicap, times on each leg but all trophies reflected that the race was to be sailed on the basis that the fastest is best.

As 1975 passed so the economic gloom cleared a little, but not sufficiently quickly or completely to encourage those on the edge of entering the race to commit themselves; even those committed were having problems in finding the finance they would need. One casualty was the team of young Frenchmen building their yacht near Paris, though they almost met their own deadline. The crew of servicemen aboard *Great Britain II*, now divided into the two crews that would sail the two stages of the race, was still short of funds. All those who were to sail in the race had decided to put a full month's pay towards the project, this raising about £5,000, and other help had come from other sources but one heavy dose of help from a commercial or industrial source was desperately needed.

6 The Festival of Sail

As the summer of 1975 passed there seemed little that the Clipper Race organizers could do which had not already been thought of. St Katherine's Dock, immediately below Tower Bridge in London, and recently turned into a yacht haven and headquarters of the new World Trade Centre, provided a magnificent centre of the Festival that was improved even further as the yachts and tall ships began to arrive in the Thames during the last week of August.

Three Clipper Race yachts, *Great Britain II*, *CS e RB II* and *The Great Escape*, were already berthed in St Katherine's alongside many famous yachts from the history of sailing including the winner of the first Fastnet Race, *Jolie Brise*, Robin Knox-Johnston's *Suhaili* and many veterans from the early days of ocean racing as we know it today.

Out in the Thames the vast square riggers began assembling. Russia's *Tovarisch* lay alongside Portugal's *Sagres* below Tower Bridge while above the bridge the German *Gorch Fock* berthed on H.M.S. *Belfast* and across the river the Danish training ship *Georg Stage* took centre stage and gave daily demonstrations of sail-setting to the delight of the thousands of people from London and the world over who saw the greatest free show London had given for years.

Britain was represented by the two Sail Training Association schooners *Sir Winston Churchill* and *Malcolm Miller*, the Sea Cadet Corps brigantine *Royalist* and several yachts from other sail training schemes, notably the Ocean Youth Club and various sailing trusts that provide opportunities of sailing to young people.

The arrival of the ships and yachts, the miles of coloured bunting that flew from masts and yards and the continual coming and going of the hundreds of workboats and launches that served them provided a never-ending spectacle, but, perhaps, none of this would have been quite the same had it not been for the weather, so often an unknown quantity during the British summer.

The Festival started on August Bank Holiday at the beginning of a heatwave that was to last until the entire fleet headed down stream at the end of the ceremonies a week later. Each dawn broke with clear blue skies and at sunset each evening, as the sun descended almost between the arches of Tower Bridge and through the rigging of countless ships, scenes emerged that kept photographers and sightseers enraptured. Meanwhile the hundreds of young men and girls who made up the crews of the training ships were entertained ashore by youth clubs, the Greater London Council and countless other wellwishers. The normally rather aloof and rule-conscious river police became ferries for the crews, often working for hours outside their normal duty so crews could go ashore or return aboard in the early hours after a night in London. In St Katherine's Haven itself there was everything that a yachtsman expects while ashore. The yacht club almost broke at the seams when the hundreds of yachtsmen in the little harbour were joined by hundreds more escaping from their London offices for a moment of respite. Added to this already cheerful confusion, thousands more sightseers joined the endless queues round the yachts, and out in the river there was almost always something new to see, be it the companies of the City of London rowing races in Thames skiffs or demonstrations of life-saving equipment.

Ashore there were sightseeing tours, almost continuously, for the cadets and trainees as well as football matches and an inter-ship tug of war in the moat of the Tower of London. Thames barges, twenty-five of them, raced up river from the estuary to Tower Bridge, helped by a kindly easterly wind and providing a timeless sight for those lining the banks of the Thames from the start to the finish. The Royal Marines with traditional precision and pomp performed the ceremony of Beating the Retreat and Sunset alongside the Tower. Mayors of the London boroughs visited the ships. The entire cadet contingent marched through the City to the Guildhall to receive prizes from the Lord Mayor of London, causing the biggest traffic jam in the City since the Coronation of the Queen, but no one seemed to mind.

Following all the spectacle, celebration and festivity the curtain began to be rung down on the scene as the week drew to a close and the start of the Clipper Race from Sheerness approached, but the Germans aboard their 1,700-ton barque *Gorch Fock* prematurely stole the scene with their departure from the Upper Pool. Leaving at the lowest point of the tide she was able to clear Tower Bridge with twenty-one inches

16.   The Danish training ship *Danmark* manoeuvring below Tower Bridge, London, during the Festival of Sail

17, 18, 19. The young crew of the Danish training ship *Georg Stage* entertained thousands of spectators each morning during the Festival by setting and furling sails while on a mooring opposite the Tower of London immediately above Tower Bridge

17

18

between the top of her main mast and the upper permanant span of the bridge and with less than three feet of water under her keel. She left under almost full sail and her crew manning the side cheered and were cheered in turn by the crews of the other square riggers as she passed down stream. It was a fine sight.

On the final Friday of the Festival the Clipper Race yachts prepared to leave, although it seemed the French yacht *Kriter II* would never be ready for the start on Sunday; aboard the other three yachts all seemed well, and their crews were itching to go. That Friday evening, the four yachts moved to the north-west corner of the dock and at a special reception on the quayside the four crews were presented to Princess Alexandra and Angus Ogilvy. Earlier in the week the same site had been used by the French when the Bishop of Beaune arrived from France to give the yacht his blessing. The Royal reception, held in perfect summer weather, was the forerunner of the Clipper Race Ball, held later that evening in the Painted Hall at the Royal Naval College, Greenwich, itself a fitting site and event to herald the start of the longest ocean race ever staged and to mark the end of a week of maritime festivity that Londoners and others will never forget.

During the early hours of Saturday, the final farewells were made and the last procession down river began. The vast convoy was led by the guard-ship for the Festival and the start of the Clipper Race, H.M.S. *London-derry*. It was appropriate, even if sad for photographers, that the fleet sailed on a morning showing the first signs of autumn, grey with a trace of light rain and mist. The procession, witnessed by hundreds of people some afloat, some on the banks of the Thames, lasted more than two hours. As the warships, the tall ships and the Clipper Race yachts passed Greenwich they passed two ships that had in their time caused a stir on the river. *Cutty Sark*, her masts towering over those of the passing ships, almost seemed to nod in approval as they went by, while in her shadow one could feel that the spirit of Sir Francis Chichester was watching from the cockpit of his yacht *Gipsy Moth IV*, ashore for ever, the Cape of Good Hope and Cape Horn behind her but the name of her owner and herself as boldly printed in the history of sail as that of the famous clipper alongside.

20.   East meets west. Two German-built training barques, the Russian *Tovarishch* and the Portuguese *Sagres* moored alongside one another for the Festival

21.   The most modern of the training barques, the German *Gorch Fock*, heads down the Thames for the open sea and passes sailing barges racing from Gravesend to Tower Bridge

22.   A salute from the present to the past. *Danmark* passes the *Cutty Sark* on her way down river. Many of the training ships dipped their ensigns to the famous old clipper as they passed on their way to sea

7 Leave the Cape of Good Hope to Port

When the convoy of training ships, commercial craft, Royal Naval vessels and the Clipper Race contestants had headed down river in the mists of Saturday 30 August, the Thames at Tower Bridge seemed strangely empty. The Thames Estuary was shrouded in grey as the four Clipper Race yachts moored off Sheerness to await the Sunday start. Families and friends took every available room in Sheerness, a small town and commercial port at the north-west tip of the Isle of Sheppey which faces across the Thames and the entrance to the River Medway. The French sail training ship *Bel Espoir* accompanied the yachts, providing help for the French crew of *Kriter* who were still struggling with last-minute tasks and completing work on the accommodation below decks.

The Dutch, the British and the Italians were as ready as ever they might have been, although there always seemed to be one more task to complete.

The start, to be signalled at 9 a.m. from H.M.S. *Londonderry* by Mr Edward Heath, was timed to give the yachts maximum benefit from the ebbing tide which would help them out to sea past North Foreland and through the Downs into the English Channel. Sunday 31 August dawned with no let-up in the autumnal weather; a chilly north easterly wind blew across the flat shores of the Thames and there was little colour for the photographers. H.M.S. *Londonderry* was anchored at the southern end of the starting line soon after dawn and the four yachts, surrounded by a fleet of small and large spectator craft, headed for sea as Mr Heath arrived by launch from Burnham-on-Crouch where he was competing in Burnham Week aboard *Morning Cloud*.

Naval launches and cutters from Trinity House took the invited spectators out to the guardship while other yachts and motor cruisers appeared through the thinning mist to join those already thronging the starting area. Last of the competing yachts to leave her anchorage was *Kriter*. Mike Gill and his crew aboard *Great Britain* were in the start-ing area early, accompanied by the Italians and the Dutch who were

47

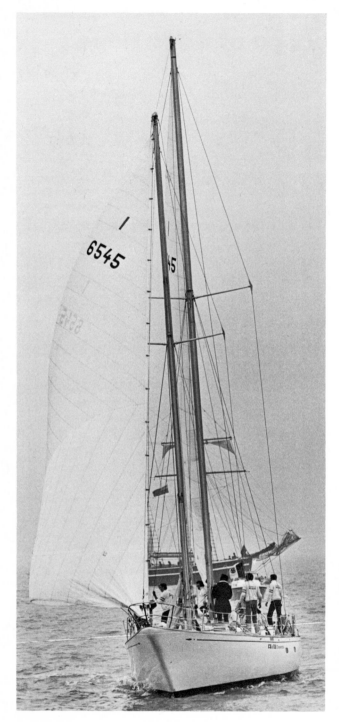
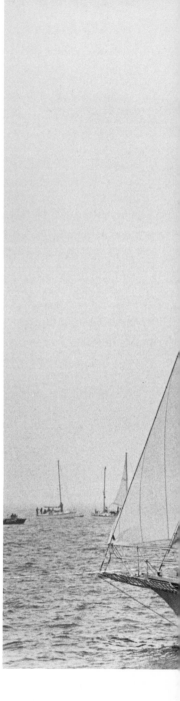

23.   The Italian schooner *CS e RB II* just prior to the start
with the French training ship *Belle Espoir* astern

24.   The Dutch ketch *The Great Escape* gybing round just before the start. The troublesome
       strengthening battens can be seen in the deck-house windows

25. Lady Sheila Chichester protects her ears from the
sound of the naval saluting guns used to start the Clipper Race

26. Mr Edward Heath gives the signal for the start of the
Clipper Race from H.M.S. *Londonderry* at 09.20, British
Summer Time, 31 August 1975

supported by a large contingent from their sailing school who had sailed to London in a yacht even smaller than *The Great Escape*.

As 8.30 approached it became clear that the French were far from ready and as they closed with the race officials aboard H.M.S. *Londonderry* the chairman of the race committee, John Roome, asked if they needed more time. Olivier de Kersauson then came alongside the warship asking for matches and an emergency liferaft radio. Not only were matches and radio produced, but he was given a postponement of ten minutes and at 8.50, when the ten-minute signal should have been fired, a double gun was fired and the postponement indicated by signal flags. In spite of this *Great Britain II*, *CS e RB II* and *The Great Escape* shaped for the starting line. When the gun fired at nine o'clock, indicating the original starting time, *Kriter II* was just clearing the warship and the others were sailing fast towards the east under the impression that the race had started. Radio messages were broadcast but still the three yachts charged onwards until recalled by spectator craft.

It was a cruel moment at such a tense time and hardly a problem needed at a moment when nerves were stretched to the limit, but the yachts came back and at 9.10 a.m. the second ten-minute warning was fired, followed at 9.15 by the five-minute gun and finally at 9.20 by the starting gun.

At least 13,000 miles lay ahead of the yachts as they headed to the line, *Kriter II* and *Great Britain II* vying for the best starting position while the Italians and Dutch held the lead for a few moments, until passed by the two larger yachts. The spectator fleet followed them seawards as the easterly wind filled and *Great Britain* began to stretch herself to nine knots, followed by *Kriter*, her skipper Olivier de Kersauson sporting his famous red French revolutionary's hat.

One by one the followers gave up the chase and the yachts were on their own, fading into the grey horizon as crews settled down into watch-keeping patterns and began to realize that months, in some cases more than a year, of planning had become a reality. The sailing instructions were aptly terse. The Queens buoy in the Thames estuary was to be left to starboard, Cape Town to port and thence to Sydney. Distance, 13,650 miles.

Once in the open sea the yachts turned south for the Straits of Dover, spinnakers set and every other running sail flying as they swung ahead of the freshening easterly wind and a brightening sky.

27. Prior to the second postponed start, *Great Britain II* heads back across the line after the first recall while *Kriter II*, foreground, prepares to hoist sail

28. *left* Twenty minutes after the start *Great Britain II* leads *Kriter II* by a clear quarter of a mile, surrounded by spectator craft

29. The loneliness of command. Olivier de Kersauson, skipper of *Kriter II*, with all the problems and turmoil of London behind him, sits alone in the sternsheets of his yacht after the start contemplating the enormity of the voyage ahead

The British crew opted for the inside course between the English coast and the Goodwin sands while the French decided on the more southerly route into the English Channel. In still bad visibility the cockpit crew of the British yacht suddenly noticed the depth indicated by their depth recorder falling fast as they approached the Quorn buoy. Realizing that they were fast approaching shoal water they gybed the yacht all standing and clawed back into deeper water but not before the recorded depth below the waterline was as little as eight feet, and this in a yacht drawing nine feet. The angle of heel had saved them from a drastic grounding on an ebbing tide. The navigator, John Bagnall, attributed the fault to the impossibility of making a good visual navigation fix from known points ashore. The compass, also, was almost certainly giving inaccurate readings as it had not been swung since the many stores and items had been loaded aboard in London. The yacht lost little time, but had the crew on deck been less alert the story might have been very different.

Although chaos still reigned below decks, the French crew soon settled to their two-watch system as they swept south-westwards, holding a mid Channel course astern of the British. The Italians took a more northerly track but with a fresh wind from astern there was little tactical thinking required before the Bay of Biscay. The shortest distance was the straight line.

It was apparent from the start that there would be no quarter between the French and the British; after 24 hours *Great Britain II* led the way down Channel, having covered 187 miles in 24 hours and 40 minutes. She was sighted 30 miles south of the Needles running under her largest spinnaker through calm seas. Twenty-five miles astern, and slightly to the north the Italians were making fast progress while the Dutch seemed to have missed the tide at Dover and were sighted by Dungeness coast guards still making slow headway along the Kent coast. The French, meanwhile, kept radio silence. They were not sighted but were thought to be south of the British and making similar progress. But that night, 2–3 September, the wind fell lighter and while *Great Britain II* dropped from an average speed of better than 7.5 knots, *Kriter* reported that she was to the west of Guernsey, twenty-four miles astern of *Great Britain II* but ahead of *CS e RB II* which was close to the Channel Islands and also struggling in the dying wind.

The problem was a high-pressure area over Cape Finisterre and the leaders made only 120 miles in the next 24 hours, averaging only 5 knots;

30.   Into the north east Trades. *Great Britain II* sighted from
a Nimrod aircraft off Finisterre, north-west Spain sailing fast
to the south-west

31. *Kriter II*, within miles of *Great Britain II* off Finisterre,
but on the opposite gybe to the British yacht and holding a
more southerly course

they were not helped by mist patches in the approaches to the Channel, particularly as they were in the busy shipping route to the northeast of Ushant. The wind stayed light during the third day and again the yachts lost time; *Patriarch*, by contrast, had gone down Channel on a fresh easterly 'under a cloud of canvas' and had been running at times at 12 knots. On this day the British crew sighted the French to the south off their port bow. It was thought that the French, reluctant as usual to report a position, might try and run through the Chenal du Four, between Ushant and the French mainland. It was, after all, Olivier de Kersauson's home territory.

As they approached the turn into Biscay on the third day the tide, which had kept *Great Britain II* frustratingly pegged to the north of the peninsula, turned and *Kriter* and *Great Britain II* were close as they entered the Bay of Biscay in darkness early on the fourth day. The fresher easterly winds returned and both were sighted on the fifth day thundering into the Atlantic off Cape Finisterre in moderate seas and making a good 10 knots. They crossed the Bay in under two full days, *Great Britain II* taking the more westerly track while the French passed almost within sight of the Spanish coast. About 150 miles behind them, the Italians were sailing fast while the Dutch crew of *The Great Escape* had put into Plymouth for repairs to damaged batteries; they lost 24 hours acquiring replacements but they doggedly sailed for Biscay as the leaders were well past the northern coast of Spain and approaching the tropics.

At the end of the first week *Great Britain II* and *Kriter II* were still level, making good progress southwestwards. As they passed the latitude of Cape St Vincent the British yacht was 150 miles further out into the Atlantic than the French. The Italians, steering a course straight from Ushant to Cape Finisterre, were 200 miles or more astern. *The Great Escape* had reached the northwestern point of the Iberian peninsula.

Patriarch's equivalent position was still ahead of the leaders but the initial gap was closing as the British crew sighted the Canary Islands to the east, aware that the French were almost certainly in among the islands, mere peaks in the distance. From this point the two tracks converged as they sailed on southwards to the Cape Verde Archipelago in the northeasterly trade winds.

Kriter was passing between Tenerife and Grand Canaria when the British saw the islands away to the east, and both yachts were making a fast passage towards the unreliable winds of the Doldrums that lie off the coast of Senegal and Guinea. The track of the yachts ran parallel towards the Cape Verde islands, sailing through clear skies and shoals of flying fish. As they approached the Cape Verdes at the end of the second week at sea *Great Britain* was heading for the most westerly islands of St Anthony and St Vincent while *Kriter* was set to pass well to the east of the most easterly island, both yachts bettering runs of 200 miles a day.

When the leaders were passing the islands and as *Great Britain* broke through the humid tropical squalls of the Cape Verdes the Italians were still maintaining a good average speed further north and passing the Canaries. The Dutch were still very much the rearguard, more than a day behind the Italians. Once through the islands Mike Gill and John Bagnall, with the help of the morse code weather details collected by Keith Powell, altered *Great Britain*'s course onto a more easterly track, closing with *Kriter* and sighting shoals of whales that leapt from the water to take a better view of the yacht.

The Doldrums were not such a great problem to either crew as they might have feared, but they did take their toll of the daily averages. After the alternating calms and storms of the Cape Verdes, *Great Britain II* took a 500-mile hitch to the south-south-east and must have almost been in sight of the French as they began to feel the end of the Doldrums and the first of the southeasterly winds beyond them. *Great Britain II* was the more easterly of the two yachts, now running parallel about fifty miles apart. On 19 September the crew of *Kriter II* sighted the top of the sails of *Great Britain II*, just ahead.

Radio contact between the yachts was becoming more frequent and less stilted, but to confirm his suspicions that he had sighted the British yacht, Olivier de Kersauson tricked Mike Gill into relaying his true position while himself passing a false position, well to the east, back to the British crew. After this brief sighting the tracks diverged again, *Great Britain II* maintaining a course to the south hard on the wind while the French, unable to point as high as the British, headed to the west of south. By the twenty-second day they were further south than *Great Britain* but 200 miles to the west. Both were still a little more than a day behind the equivalent distance sailed by the clipper *Patriarch* on her maiden voyage to Australia during that winter 106 years earlier.

At this point radio contact with Doi Malingri and his crew aboard

1. A forest of masts in the Pool of London.
    Sunset during the Festival of Sail

2. Shaking a reef out of *Great Britain*'s mainsail as the wind eases a little on the approach through the north-east Trades to the Doldrums and the equator

2

3. A masthead view of the deck of *Great Britain II* in a moderate following wind
4. *Great Britain*'s foredeck crew take in a headsail as the wind freshens in the southern Atlantic
5. Retrieving a spinnaker that had been overrun by *Great Britain II* in the south Indian Ocean

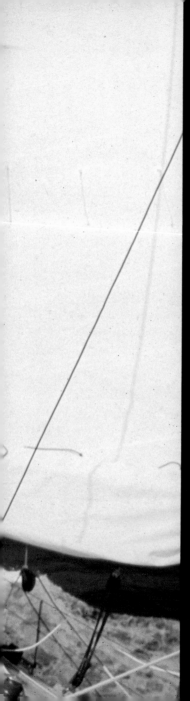

3

4

6. The first landfall since leaving the northern Atlantic.
The coast of Victoria, Australia, as *Great Britain II*
passes through the Bass Strait and into the
Pacific Ocean

32.   Hoisting a head sail in mid ocean. Sail changing
required a complete watch on deck and often the help of the
stand-by watch

33.   Brigadier John Bagnall, who retired from the Army on
the day before the start of the race. His expertise both as
navigator and as weather forecaster played a vital part in the
success of *Great Britain II* in the leg from London to Sydney

34, 35. The vital ingredients of offshore navigation:
azimuth tables, an accurate watch, dividers and a plotting
sheet. The positions on the chart table show that *Great
Britain II* was near the Kerguelen Islands, in the Southern
Ocean, when the picture was taken

CS e RB II was lost. Her last report was that she was passing the Cape Verde islands seventeen days after the start. Then there was silence and attempts by *Great Britain II* to establish a link failed (*Great Britain II* had been relaying positions of the other yachts to London). While there was no anxiety about the *CS e RB II* at this stage the weather in the area was checked in London and after the silence had lasted a week shipping was asked to keep a look-out and report any sightings to Lloyds in London.

The silence of the Italians might be attributed to several possible factors. The cause could have been a straightforward radio failure or a complete failure of the electrical system could have cut off power for either the main radio or the emergency set. Dismasting could have destroyed the tri-atic aerials. It seemed unlikely that the yacht had been run-down or had simple foundered; but after ten days of silence, and no sighting of the yacht either near the Cape Verde islands, or to the south, the first steps were put in hand to coordinate a search. These steps did not involve any maritime organization other than those already available, such as long-range military or naval reconnaissance aircraft already patrolling the area, merchant shipping and military vessels. Thirteen days after her last call the yacht was seen by the Libyan-owned Liberian tanker, the 47,000-ton *Ras Lanuf*. She reported sighting the yacht 500 miles northeast of the north coast of Brazil; all appeared well aboard but no radio contact was made indicating that the problems certainly stemmed from the radio itself.

By now the navigators of the leading two yachts were approaching a crucial time. On *Great Britain II* radio operator Keith Powell was reading the high-speed morse signals sent out from weather centres which he 'translated' and plotted onto a special chart to provide a complete weather map of the ocean ahead. This weather 'fax' (facsimile) system showed the South Atlantic high-pressure area to be moving very slowly east; therefore the calm in the centre of the area would be nearer to the African coast than expected.

This weather information is available to any yacht with the equipment to receive it; the morse signal is so fast that the crew of the British yacht *Adventure* in the last race around the world had tape-recorded the signals and then replayed them at a slower speed. Keith Powell was able to read the morse 'live', and using the weather map John Bagnall and Mike Gill decided on a course that was something of a calculated gamble but which certainly won them the first leg of the race. They started their turn to the southeast on 27 September while *Kriter II*, 200 miles to the west and still sailing just west of a due southerly course, continued southwards.

The British crew had already heard from position reports that the French had crossed the equator on 21 September well to the west; this showed they could sail closer to the wind than the French, an added help to beating them across the South Atlantic and into the Roaring Forties for the turn towards Australia.

On 27 September, while sailing southeast, the speed of *Great Britain II* slowed a little and she had to keep tacking to maintain her intended best course. The French continued southwards on port tack until 30 September, when, at a latitude of almost 30 degrees south and a longitude of 30 degrees west, they turned southeast, feeling the first push of the cold southerly air stream from the Antarctic. The courses of the two yachts described graceful arcs into the Southern Ocean and both yachts entered the latitude of the Roaring Forties between 6 and 7 October, set to pass well south of Cape Town. The British claimed they were leading while the French pointed out, possibly correctly, that they were nearer to Sydney on the Great Circle route across the Southern Ocean.

Astern, *The Great Escape* continued her straight course to the south, now almost 2,000 miles behind *Great Britain II* but following her track closely.

The Italians had put into Recife, Brazil, for essential repairs to their radio as they had to broadcast their position to London when they crossed the compulsory stop-line that stretched from Rio across the Atlantic to the east. Failure to broadcast on crossing a stop-line or to report from nominated ports after such a failure would have led to disqualification.

The Englishman aboard the yacht, Geoff Cross, telephoned the London race office from Recife sounding desperately disappointed. He told the race organizers that they had enjoyed some superb sailing and that the winds had never failed. They were in Recife several days waiting for the unhurried South Americans to effect repairs; Cross summing up the first leg of the race from London to Sydney later said that the most dangerous part of the voyage had been a bus ride in Recife. They were determined to continue once repairs were complete and hoped to catch the Dutch who were now well on their way to the Southern Ocean.

The next stop-line, at which it was compulsory for the yachts to report their position, ran due south from Cape Town. *Great Britain II* crossed this mark at first light on 9 October after a 24-hour run of 230 miles. They were 450 miles south of the Cape and were thus unable to make a rendezvous which had been planned with a ship and aircraft of the South African armed forces. *Kriter II* crossed the stop line 20 hours later 200 miles south of the British.

Once past Cape Town and Cape Agulhas the chase between the two leaders really began, but east of this line *Kriter II* hit, literally, a problem which contributed to her arriving second at Sydney. While sailing fast in fresh following winds she hit a whale, on the surface of the ocean, probably asleep. Julian Gildersleeve, the Englishman sailing aboard the yacht, said it was like riding a bicycle at full speed into a brick wall. The yacht stopped in her tracks; the whale, almost certainly fatally wounded, dived leaving a trail of blood, while water flowed into the yacht through a hole below the waterline on the starboard bow.

What might have happened if the bow had not been strengthened by the French before the start, an improvement on the strengthening added by Leslie Williams two years earlier in Port Elizabeth, hardly bears consideration. Apart from the gash and a dent above the waterline, the damage was relatively minor and contained by a watertight compartment in the bow; the water taken on required only fifteen minutes pumping each day.

At this point *Great Britain II*, not experiencing the ferocious winds expected in the southern latitudes, was about 120 miles ahead of the French. Both yachts were now inside the record set by *Patriarch*, and it dawned on Mike Gill and his crew that the record was beatable, in spite of the pessimism of some of those at home.

Astern, still in the South Atlantic, another chase was developing. The Italians aboard *CS e RB II* had left Recife on 5 October and were in hot pursuit of the Dutch aboard *The Great Escape*. A week after leaving Brazil the Italians were about two days astern of the Dutch who were approaching the Forties latitude and beginning their turn east.

Ahead the fresher winds, and the strain of continual fast sailing, were taking their toll of the sails aboard *Great Britain II* and Mike Gill signalled home to London that extensive sail repair and replacement would be needed in Sydney. Many of the sails aboard *Great Britain II* had already been round the world once and even the heavy spinnakers, called bullet-proof by the enigmatic servicemen, were breaking up. One headsail had been given to the yacht, with a quantity of cash and some fine Havana cigars, by the British distributors of Punch Havanas, and this was doing sterling work as the expected westerlies seemed continually to fade and swing to the east. The cost of sail replacements was thought to be about £10,000, serious news for the crew aboard, the crew waiting to replace them and the project organizers already worried about the debts of the scheme.

Olivier de Kersauson had not reported a position since passing South Africa's longitude but was thought to be holding a more southerly course than the British. On Trafalgar Day, 21 October, positions received from both yachts showed that *Great Britain II* had a lead of about 200 miles, or about one day. Both yachts reported daily runs of better than 200 miles. Between the Îles Crozet and the Îles Kerguelen, at 50 degrees south, the French had been completely headed by the wind and for some time had actually sailed away from Australia on a northerly heading.

While approaching the longitude of the Îles Crozet the French crew were aware that their main compass was not giving as accurate a course reading as they might have wished, but the extent of the inaccuracy was not known. When rushing eastwards on the front of a westerly gale, carrying heavy spinnaker and reduced mainsail at night, one of the watch on deck took a look ahead into the darkness and to his horror saw the vague outline of land only a short distance away. One of the Crozet Islands, supposedly miles to the south, lay dead ahead. The yacht was swung to port all standing and with a headsail hoisted to smother the flogging spinnaker the French clawed their way to the northwest against the wind, losing several hours and never sure just how close they had come to running onto an uninhabited island in one of the least hospitable parts of the world.

In London and Sydney, those plotting the positions of the yachts from their radio messages were often under the impression that the leaders were sailing more than 300 miles in 24 hours. However, both John Bagnall and Yves Olivaux, when comparing their notes and log books

36, 37. Recovering a torn spinnaker aboard *Great Britain II*. Weakness in the metal swivel fittings at the masthead led to the sail flying free; then it was often overrun and lost as the yacht sailed over it. Dennis Cooke, a Naval Airman, spent many hours stitching torn sails either in the old-fashioned way with needle and palm or, when practicable, with a manually operated sewing-machine

38. Working one of the two 'coffee-grinder' winches aboard *Great Britain II*. Even the skipper, Mike Gill, was not exempt from this back-breaking work

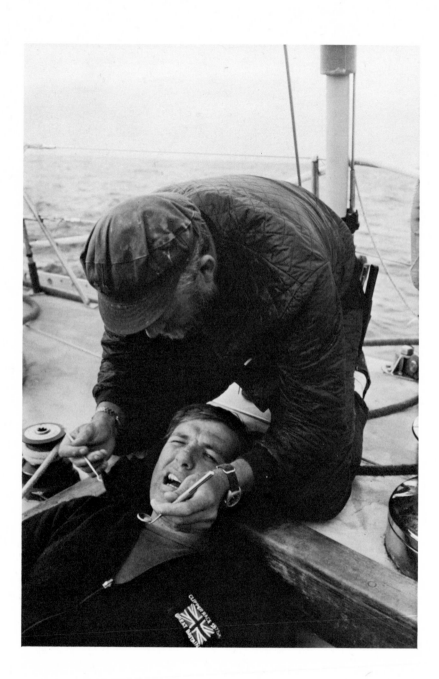

39.   One of the hazards of sailing. Chief Naval Medical
Technician John Parfoot fills a tooth for Colin Wagstaff. The
operation was a complete success in spite of the scanty
facilities

after arrival in Australia, realized that neither yacht had made a daily run of more than approximately 280 miles. The uncertainty was a result of sailing conditions. An accurate daily fix from the sun or stars was often impossible and dead reckonings had to be made for the position instead. These were made by using the hourly entries of speed in the log and the readings for the day on the electric logs. The latter are worked by underwater impellers and when a yacht is rolling and pitching wildly the readings can be slightly inaccurate. Unless some danger lies ahead yachtsmen assume these calculations to be on the pessimistic side. Once an accurate position fix became possible again the aggregate distance from the last accurate fix could be plotted. The aggregate could, for example, be 800 miles in three days, an impressive total – but had an accurate fix been possible in the intervening times, it might have shown widely differing runs for each of the three days, say two of 300 and one of 200.

In fact, *Great Britain II* probably had three daily runs of about 260 miles. This is an impressive daily run in anyone's terms, an average of about 11 knots, and there were times in the Southern Ocean when the leaders were surfing ahead of following winds at an indicated 20 knots. In one of the few severe storms encountered in the Southern Ocean on this leg, near Kerguelen Island, *Great Britain II* surfed for a period at 20 knots carrying only a number 3 headsail, but this weather with winds of 60 knots and more was the exception rather than the rule. In the earlier race around the world Chay Blyth and his team had reported similar experiences and it was in these waters and storms that the Mexican yacht *Sayula* was virtually capsized. But this time, for the leaders, the Forties failed to roar though both the Italians and the Dutch had to weather several heavy storms further astern when they came through later.

While the leaders approached the longitude of west Australia five days ahead of *Patriarch*'s relative position it was becoming increasingly apparent that the 69-day record could be broken. The yachts needed to reach Sydney by 8 November and both were within 1,500 miles of the finishing line with 9 days in hand.

While *Great Britain* on latitude 46 south and *Kriter* on latitude 42 south began heading to the north for the Bass Strait, between Tasmania and the Australian mainland, *The Great Escape* was passing the stop-line on the Cape Town longitude, still following the track of *Great Britain II*.

40, 41.   Night in the Southern Ocean, David Leslie, who sailed both legs,
is at the helm with skipper Mike Gill to his right. Foul-weather gear was
vital to the efficiency and success of the *Great Britain*. Safety harness
was always worn (inset) and, whenever practicable, attached to the
lifelines at night and in heavy weather

CS e RB II had caught her and was almost on the same line of longitude but several degrees further south. She went further south than any of the others on the first leg, reaching 51 degrees south when passing the western Australian stop-line, but while these crews battled bravely onwards the spotlight was centring on the leaders as they fought out the final miles.

The Bass Strait, a dangerous navigation area even in good weather, gave the crews their first taste of storms for some time. As *Kriter II* made for the Strait to pass north of King Island in the approaches, *Great Britain II* kept south of the island while an intense area of low pressure settled over the east end of the Strait. As this area of storm passed over the Strait it caught *Great Britain II* on the wrong side and she had to tack to make the Strait while *Kriter* was freed and made up considerable distance. *Great Britain II* then found herself in the centre of the storm area and was becalmed before the wind returned with a vengeance. She left the Strait with her lead cut to about 150 miles and headed northwards towards Sydney, keeping close to the coast to avoid the worst of the south-running current offshore but risking the calms that lurk off the headlands along the eastern Australian coastline.

While passing Wilson's Promontory, the most southeastern point of the Australian mainland to the north of Flinder's Island, the British crew were approached by several young people in an outboard driven dory.

'Where have you come from?' shouted the Australians, the first people the British crew had seen since their last sight of *Kriter* six weeks earlier.

'London,' shouted the crew.

'Oh yer?' replied the Australians, and motored away.

Both yachts were through the Bass Strait and on the final leg north with four days in hand against the 106-year-old record. Each lighthouse and headland reported their progress as they passed, though the French, further offshore, were sighted less often.

As the night of 5 November settled over the Australian Pacific coast the British were making slow progress along the shore while the French made better time out to sea, reducing the British lead every hour by several miles. *Great Britain*'s crew finally sighted the towering cliffs north of Sydney Harbour entrance, but as night fell the coast breezes were dying. Only a mile from the finishing line and surrounded by spectator craft she came to a complete halt, her largest lightest spinnaker hanging lifeless from the mast and the ocean swell doing nothing to help her progress.

Kriter II, still out at sea, was making 7 knots a mere 40 miles from the finish. While camera arc lights dazzled the frustrated British crew an Australian journalist shouted to Mike Gill 'What do you want most of all after 67 days at sea?' to which the laconic skipper of the British yacht, his mind far from the nubile delights of Sydney which were apparently on the mind of the Australian, replied, 'To finish the bloody race.'

The British waited in agony, knowing that the French were still moving well offshore. After almost two hours *Great Britain* began to move once more and at 2.38 on the morning of 7 November they crossed the finishing line as the breeze filled in from the sea. The same breeze was carrying *Kriter II* with it and surrounded by an impressive fleet she crossed the line at 9.07 the same morning to be greeted by an already-jubiliant British crew and a band of the Royal Australian Navy.

All times for the race were based on Greenwich and the actual finishing times were 15.38.49 hours and 22.07.00 hours respectively on 6 November, giving *Great Britain* a time for the distance of 67 days 7 hours 18 minutes 9 seconds, and for *Kriter* 67 days 13 hours 47 minutes 20 seconds. *Patriarch*'s record was broken for ever and among the welcoming crowd witnessing the arrival was Diana Plater, the great-grand-daughter of Captain Henry Plater, one of the former captains of *Patriarch*.

One moment during the arrival scenes in Sydney came as something of a surprise not only to the crew of *Great Britain II*, but, more particularly, her navigator John Bagnall. Among those aboard the awaiting small craft at the finish as well as his wife was his daughter Jane who he had not expected in the family reunion. But the reunion was not entirely and exclusively family, for unknown to her father, Jane had become engaged to the photographer aboard the yacht, Captain Ian Kirkwood of the Royal Corps of Transport, and her father only then realized that he had just spent 67 days at sea with his future son-in-law.

While the leading crews were celebrating and relaxing ashore, life was different back in the Southern Ocean to the southeast of Cape Town. *The Great Escape* had met a depression, or, more accurately, had been caught by one moving from the west, of 978 millibars. Depression seemed to be

42. *Kriter II* from the air eight miles north-east of
Merrimbula making about six knots; the photograph was
taken by a Royal Australian Navy plane on a morning sortie

43, 44. *Great Britain II* approaches the finish off Sydney
accompanied by Albert Ross, a seabird who followed her for
several days in the Southern Ocean

following depression and this was a low as any, bringing fog, rain and freezing conditions with winds of up to 60 knots. As the French and British, who had only met two storms during the entire voyage, enjoyed Sydney sunshine, the Dutch were fighting to save a sail that had been washed overboard in mountainous seas. The sail, trapped beneath the hull, was rescued only by lowering Bart-Jan van Gronenberg over the side as the bow of the yacht plunged into the seas, often buried.

Day after day the story from the Dutch was the same, storms, gales and a life of wet misery below decks. Sjerp Noorda fell from the mast during one storm and badly bruised his ribs and was confined to his bunk in great pain for several days. The nightmare continued from early November until the end of the month by which time Henk Huisman, the skipper, reported that morale was dropping and that he was having to drive the crew out on deck to work. The continual bad weather was causing health problems. Eyes were affected by the salt and cuts were not healing properly. During the height of one storm on 27 November, south of the western coast of Australia, the crew had fears for themeslves and their yacht, but both survived while the Italians, already through the Bass Strait and heading for Sydney, were predicting that they would reach the finish on 30 November.

The problems aboard *CS e RB II* were different. The stop at Recife had extended their voyage and food was virtually finished when they were still two weeks out, but this problem was yet to be known in Sydney as their radio reporting was sparse in the extreme.

As the Italians finished after 2,194 hours at sea the weather eased for the Dutch, now crossing the Great Bight south of Australia. Their morale rose with the warmer conditions. Incredibly radio messages from the yacht were still being relayed through Ijmuiden, in Holland, to the race control centre in Sydney and late on the night of 10 December, after 103 days at sea, they reached Sydney with only one complaint. They had run out of toilet paper, surely a drastic problem for the fastidious Dutch.

8 The First Leg in Retrospect

In Australia the skipper and navigator of *Great Britain II*, Mike Gill and John Bagnall, and the skipper and navigator of *Kriter II*, Olivier de Kersauson and Yves Olivaux, were invited to a special dinner. Host at the dinner was Anthony Churchill, one of the two people who originally conceived the race, and the other guests included Australian yachting writer Peter Campbell and the skipper of *Great Britain II* for the return leg to Britain, Roy Mullender. The conversation at the dinner, ranging over various aspects of the race, was based on a few basic questions from Anthony Churchill. Otherwise it was spontaneous, and the track of the interview unplanned. The discussion was tape-recorded; extracts from it follow:

Churchill: One of the race rules indicates that the organizers would take it very hard if a crewman was lost and was not using a harness. Any comments?

Gill: I certainly believe that on calm nights you're just as much at risk if not more so, so we encouraged the harness's use in light as well as heavy weather.

de Kersauson: It is very difficult to talk about that because if people know you are not wearing a harness and an accident happens, everybody says 'Ah, he should have been wearing a harness.' But if you wear a harness all the time then you'll manoeuvre like a pig.

Gill: Yes, but a lot of our training did involve moving around the ship with a harness on, so that the crew were used to it. On occasions, it is slower. There were occasions when we would dash on deck and would not use a harness immediately.

de Kersauson: Harnesses are at some point quite dangerous because you have to run very fast. You are on the foredeck in your harness and you break a guy on the spinnaker. Have you seen this happen? If you are in your harness, you can't run – you are tied like a dog. I think the idea of harnesses is O.K. for some things. I ask my crew to put it on sometimes, but I don't agree with a permanent harness because if there is a crash or an accident and you are in harness, you are just trapped. But I watch my crew extremely closely as they manoeuvre around the deck but I don't want to make them 'sissy' in mind.

Gill: It all boils down to the Skipper's responsibility in the end. He must justify his way of sailing the boat.

de Kersauson: Justify to whom?

Gill: Himself.

de Kersauson: Yes, and that's what I do, in my conscience. I think that safety is more a matter of boat preparation: good non-slip surfaces on the deck. Good winches for gybing. That is good safety: prevention of accidents. The harness is not preventive. The harness is a point behind an accident, if you know what I mean. And if you do wear a harness you must have a 'true' harness, not one from the chest. I have been in the water at 10 knots to give myself an idea of the feeling a man has of being dragged with a chest harness on. It is a very wet feeling because you nearly die with all the water you absorb.

Gill: There is a case for development of the harness. It should still be able to be used on deck. In other words, used with an attachment somewhere on the chest and yet when a man goes in the water he is dragged from his back.

de Kersauson: That is the smart idea. But there is no rule when to use one. You do not wear a harness for years and then regret for ever one day not using it. But life is like that. You can smoke to forty-five and then be told you've only eight months to live.

Campbell: Mike [Gill], did you lose anybody overboard?

Gill: People were hanging over the pulpit on occasions, but at every point on the boat where people worked for a period of time, such as the pulpit, mast, or helmsman's cockpit, we had straps with carbiniere hooks on so that instead of using their own lines, they would use these, which meant their own lines were instantly available to hook on and move out, or whatever. And it also meant that the jackstay, that ran the whole length of the ship, wasn't cluttered up by other people's hooks. On one occasion, when we were dropping the large genoa . . . the practice we had was to put the boat slightly aback so that the centre of the sail came over the centre line of the foredeck and then just let the halyard run, so that the whole sail was gathered on to the foredeck. Once . . . the halyard got stuck and the boat got slightly more aback than we intended and the two people who were gathering on the foredeck were pressed on the foredeck, and the person hauling down from the pulpit was pushed over the side, but he called 'man overboard' and was hanging on with his hands. He got his feet wet but he was secured to the boat at all times. He was permanently attached and by the time the boat was under control again he was back on board and we didn't know about it until he told us later. So there was no question of anyone parting contact with the ship.

Bagnall: From my point of view, I must say I considered the safety harness more of a convenience than a necessity. If you always wear a harness, you use it according to your judgement. Sometimes it is more convenient to use it because you use it as another 'leg' to pull against and then you can do more work. And other times you don't need it and you don't use it.

Gill: We sailed this race as a Services adventure training exercise and that means that people who are on board are not all natural sailors. And they don't react in a way that a natural sailor would to an emergency or an incident, and this is where discipline and rules are far more likely to work.

I think for us the use of harnesses is a must.

Campbell: Mike, what other personal safety equipment do you have on board?

Gill: Well, we had a hand-sized distress beacon which again we didn't carry all the time but we eventually decided the best way to carry it was to strap the beacon on to the safety harness so that when the safety harness was worn, this beacon was all sewn onto it. The idea being that if a man was lost over the ship and went out of visual range, he would have this radio transponder which we could pick up from the ship with a special receiver and we could home back on him to within visual range. The instrument was proved to be reasonably accurate in home waters. But it hasn't been tried in difficult weather yet. As a Service entry we had the best equipment, and also some for us to test out for possible further use. For instance, things like mini-flares – they are quite handy as you can use them reasonably easily but they have a reputation for not being very visible, especially in high winds. They tend to fly a bit side-ways, so there is again an area for development of an easily used flare which can be carried in the pocket of an oilskin and which will not deteriorate over a period of several weeks and that can be operated single-handed by a man in the water.

We all carry torches, but a torch on a dark night in a breaking sea and spray is very difficult to see.

The best light produced so far have been the strobe lights which have been fixed to the lifebuoys to go over the side. There is room for development of an individual strobe light, but it might be rather expensive and fairly bulky. A small individual strobe light attached to oilskins would be a great improvement on the present sea activated, rather dim lights, and on lifejackets.

de Kersauson: One safety idea I'd like to see developed is a small gun which will fire a safety line.

But let me take a risk in what I'm saying. What's a liferaft's use on this race? In 55 degrees south, if you get into a liferaft you won't live to tell the tale, only prolong the suffering. That's what I believe. Security comes from action taken before a possible accident; not from 'do this, do that' instructions after an accident. My point of view is that life now is getting so security-conscious, you can't blow your nose without asking permission. I think the radio can give you security. If you need a technical problem solved, you can talk to experts ashore.

Gill: And you can get weather warnings from radios.

de Kersauson: No, it is no use hearing that you will have a 200-knot gale coming 24 hours before because it doesn't change anything except to make you a little more depressed.

Now I have a question. If you are surfing with spinnaker up, how long have you to stop your yacht when you hear 'man overboard'?

Gill: You could stop the ship in three minutes, but you would break gear.

de Kersauson: What you would do?

Gill: You'd cut the guy and put her hard up. The guy would run out through the end of the pole and the spinnaker would be streaming from the masthead with the sheet attached.

de Kersauson: But the problem is that if the sea is big, you must not have anything attached between spinnaker and yacht or she will broach. Let the halyard run too. I think it would take one hour before the boat is in condition to make a proper search.

Mullender: Can I break in here? I've been doing some research into this. In a smaller 55-foot boat. My conclusion is you've got to get rid of the guy and get the spinnaker away from the end of the pole, whether you cut it or let it run through. You then tack the boat while she has still gòt speed on and this puts you pointing back at the man in the water. You then have got to let your spinnaker halyard run through and if necessary cut it and the spinnaker will drop into the water astern. You can recover it. You can start your engine and you will be able to sail close-hauled on your mainsail back towards the man. If you know what you have to do you ought not to get more than 150 yards from the man in the water and you ought to be able to keep him in sight some of the time, even in a big sea. It's the best way I've yet developed and I think it may work but it's yet to be proven in the frightening conditions of the Southern Ocean. Let's hope we don't have to.

Churchill: Mike, can you tell us about your three-watch system?

Gill: We had a four-man, four-hour watch change and change about. The third, 'Mother Watch' is on standby ready to go on deck to help in any manoeuvre. They would also do all the cooking, cleaning and maintenance of the ship in that period. Meanwhile, the other two watches would do watch on, watch off for four hours. And at the end of that 24 hours we would swop over and one of the other watches would go into the mother watch.

Churchill: That makes four people to each watch, with skipper and navigator free of the watch system.

Gill: That's correct.

Churchill: Olivier, did you use this kind of a watch system as well?

de Kersauson: No. We used four hours on, four off every day. Two watches of five. But every day one man from each watch is what I call 'on vacation'. He sleeps all night, cleans the boat, does small repairs, eats, sleeps, reads, that's all.

Churchill: Did you have too few or too many crew for the trip? Fourteen for *G.B. II* and twelve for *Kriter.*

de Kersauson: For greatest fun, I think all you need to handle a boat of that size is eight or nine because you can do everything with seven on deck and you've plenty of room below decks. But we were very happy. We'd some twenty-year-olds and they had a lot to learn. About sailing. And about life too. Being away. And they had to learn about being with other people, too. None have been through military service where they learn how awful life can be. They're learning that with me.

Churchill: Are you going to change your crew number and system on the second leg?

de Kersauson: No.

Mullender: We're going to follow through with the same system. With our less dedicated sailors the three watches give the bit of variety. I have one nineteen-year-old. He'll get more rest than on a watch-on watch-off system.

Churchill: The rules for this race will be improved on and used as a basis for other long-distance races. Are there points in the rules which you think are stupid or should be altered or improved? Or did you just conform to them and that was that?

Gill: We managed to conform to the rules without too much effort – it would have been stupid of us to try to do anything about it. They didn't detract from the race. I know Olivier and I don't agree about radio reporting, for example. We spoke on occasions and had a different attitude.

Olivier (who evidently used it for his pranks): I see you.

Gill: Yes. That was a classic occasion. But for us it was almost a military exercise in communications, having to report once a day to England, and if we had problems in a part of the world where there were very very few if no rescue services, then the possibility of finding us was increased tremendously if we had reported. It may be that if we did report daily, then didn't, people would jump too early to the wrong conclusion. But the race did have 'stop-lines' which yachts could not pass without reporting in to the nearest port.

Campbell: If you had a choice, would you pick the same boats again for the race?

de Kersauson: I can't say because I think the only rigging interesting for this race would be a schooner, especially for safety.

Gill: But in a schooner, you cannot carry a big spinnaker . . .

de Kersauson: Yes, but I've to sail far further yet to make up my mind.

Gill: In the last round the world race I was on the ketch, *British Soldier* and now on another ketch, and Roy [Mullender] was on the sloop, *Adventure*. And I had a tremendous amount to do with the working on *Adventure*. Obviously, the Navy plugged very heavily for a cutter sloop and thinking back on our experience with a ketch then and now, I think I would go the other way and go for the cutter rig sloop.

Churchill: This is the rig that Julian Everett* drew up for a Joint Services project for this race.

Gill: If you are cruising, a ketch every time. If you are racing, if you lose one stick [mast] you are out of the race anyway. You might just as well have one stick with as much sail on as possible.

Mullender: I don't think the mizzen works any time. The boys on *Sayula* [winner of the last round the world race] certainly said that though they'd take a Swan 65 again, they'd leave their mizzen mast behind. This surprised me. But they said after the race, definitely no to two sticks.

Gill: There are obviously times when two sticks work, but the times when it pays – a broad reach – come up too seldom even on this kind of race. Going to windward in the Roaring Forties – they didn't roar this year – in light winds meant the mizzen was useless. Even downwind it wasn't earning its keep.

Campbell: Is it of value as a sail when you reef down? Say dropping your main and carrying a mizzen?

Gill: We didn't reef down that way. When you are running and you have too much sail on you take down sail from stern forward. Mizzen, mizzen stays, reef the main and finally spinnaker. Beating into a gale, we had a small headsail up; we weren't using the mizzen. On a broad reach in a gale, I would have a staysail and a reefed main to keep the effort in the middle of the ship, where it's easier to handle the sail anyway.

Our mizzen is not as well stayed as it might be anyway, and we don't have fixed back stay which is another point.

de Kersauson: In some points you must have compromise because if you are not on a ketch you need an iron man to drive her. An extra metre on the mast is a big jump, and you are eating halyards. If three or four metres higher it will be very tough on the men.

Churchill: How do you think of future long-distance races after this? O.K., you've enjoyed this but to fix up a sponsor it usually takes about one year of work. Is it worthwhile doing, and if so, what kind of long distance race do you yachtsmen want to do?

* Former editor of *Seahorse*, magazine of the Royal Ocean Racing Club.

Gill: Another like this . . . such as your projected race for the tea route from Hong Kong to Europe in 1979. I think everyone in the services is far more interested because we would not be able to compete with Admiral's Cuppers because we don't have the money or the time to produce the team for that sort of race. But in this sort of race we can come into our own because we do have skills and, now, experience to fall back on. And it's just right for adventure training.

Mullender: I would say it is desperately important to get a race's name right. The name of this race conjures up the image in people's minds of big square riggers.

I think, to be honest, it was a mistake to call it a Clipper Race, because a great many people pictured it to be a race of square riggers. I think it should have been called 'The Race against the Clippers' or a 'sea race' against the usual 'ocean race'.

Churchill: But the press would never use a longer title, would they Peter [Campbell]?

Campbell: Yes. But it's misleading.

Gill: But what about – in 1979 – getting a modern sail training ship to race against modern yachts.

Churchill: Did you have much of an advantage, Mike, having a first-class morse operator sometimes working six hours a day, writing down weather reports?

Gill: I think Olivier and I both agree: you take the weather very much as you find it, and if you are fortunate enough to get something definite about the weather you may not be able to act on it anyway. How far can you go in sailing around a weather system? It's no use chasing weather. The yacht's speed isn't fast enough.

de Kersauson: I think that sometimes a good forecast can be very important. For example, one must have the exact position of the eye of the high in the South Atlantic.

Gill: But how accurate are they? There was one time we were transferring from receiving information from one station to another and there was no continuity. So which one do you believe, or do you carry on and hope that you've chosen the right course?

Bagnall: If you plot the movement of that 'eye' as we did, it didn't behave logically. I think that ninety percent of the weather forecast information is either yesterday's, or wrong, or you know already so it's no use. Ten percent of it is useful, perhaps, and true. And of that ten percent, how much can you actually react to? One percent? Right? One time in a hundred you get something which is true and useful and you can do something, and for that one time are you going to spend £2,000 on a weather fax machine, or are you going to have two more sails?

Churchill: If you have a person who can do morse and is no sailor, the alternative is to have a weather fax and a sailor. So the fax frees one man.

Gill: Yes. But we basically did take on that 'some one' whose main skill was morse, and I think it paid off from our point of view because we did make use of the forecast on one occasion which really won us the race this far – knowing the high pressure off the South Atlantic was moving eastward rather than westward; and we were therefore able to point up and cut the corner. Olivier, not being sure, wanted to sail faster by reaching and went round the classic route, and that is where the race for us was made.

Bagnall: We had always wanted, obviously, to cut the corner as much as possible and the question was – how much information would we get to enable us to cut it by how much. Obviously, always we would have preferred to have been further east than we were.

Gill: That is one of the main advantages of our modern yachts – we can sail to windward whereas the clippers could not, and therefore we could hope to be able to modify the clipper route.

Churchill: On sailing to windward, your mainmast backstay had a hydraulic tensioner on it – *Kriter* didn't. So you could point closer to the wind than *Kriter*, and cut off that corner by more than *Kriter* could have done.

de Kersauson: Yes, that's for sure – we're not so close winded.

Churchill: But rod rigging and hydraulics are more suspect as they have less 'give' than wire: important in this type of race.

Gill: That bit of equipment from the outside looks suspect but, in fact, mechanically it is very strong. It is a hydraulically assisted screwjack. The screw takes the strain, not the hydraulics.

de Kersauson: I think you beat me by 250 miles cutting the corner, because when we went more south we were getting the wind on the nose.

Mullender: When the two yachts came down the African coast, in fact, *Kriter* was closer to the coast, which put you, in fact, eastward of the two. You then crossed over and came outboard yacht. What was the reason for that?

de Kersauson: The boat we had was on a faster point of sailing, running than *G.B. G.B.* was tacking downwind.

Gill: Were you using a Big Boy – we didn't have one?

de Kersauson: Yes. And also on *G.B. II* with long spinnaker poles. It's a job gybing so you keep the spi full and change course. With us, it's far easier to gybe. So much of our changing positions with *G.B. II* was dictated not by weather but by the different characteristics of our yachts.

Mullender: To take your point, Anthony, I think the major difference in the two boats on this leg is the fact that *G.B. II* did not have a Big Boy and *Kriter* did, and that meant that *G.B. II* really had to put the wind on the quarter instead of running dead.

Gill: This is not so in the Southern Indian Ocean because there were very few conditions when we needed a Big Boy. Going downwind generally, we surf more easily than *Kriter*; we accelerate quicker, being a lighter displacement boat. But then she can carry sail area in more acute conditions, which may mean when we are too scared to surf, she is still going.

de Kersauson: The Big Boy is like a spinnaker staysail. The times you can use it are very few. It's rather something fun to keep you busy; sometimes to give you a quarter knot more.

Did you find any magnetic anomalies en route?

Gill: No.

Bagnall: You found some?

de Kersauson: Near Crozet?

Bagnall: We were somewhere north of Crozet, but no magnetic anomaly was found and we started with a compass which had not been swung all the week. Not even in the Cape Verdes, and the chart had said to watch for magnetic anomaly. We could not find any anywhere though we sailed through the Verdes.

Mullender: Some fuss was made in the commentaries of the previous round the world race about the superior position of the modern navigator because he has all these electronic aids. Did you, in fact, find this so, or are you still using the old tools the square riggers were using? Are there great modern aids which make this so much easier?

Gill: Yves was saying that he thinks we are better equipped in particular with Brookes and Gatehouse equipment. Olivier was looking at our D.R. computer, which we never turned on, and frankly I didn't really want it aboard as it has to be very carefully calibrated if to be of any use at all, and is not for our sort of racing.

de Kersauson: We had one on *Pen Duick VI* which worked well.

Gill: But then, if you know your position within five miles, that is enough, surely? Ten miles is enough.

de Kersauson: Not always.

Gill: Oh, I mean in the middle of the ocean. Approaching land is different.

Bagnall: But generally the advantage one has is time. One knows the time; one knows one's longitude, and apart from that there are easier methods of doing the old, old things. Modern techniques – it was suggested we should take Loran, but no way. The methods used are the same as a hundred years ago.

Most of the time the accuracy to which I tried to work to was unnecessary. You didn't need it. To make a landfall you need everything you can get and, in fact, we had a star series which made all the difference to the confidence with which we made our landfall in the Bass Strait. Like everything else, you don't need it ninety percent of the time, but when the ten percent comes up you've got it. But the methods are the same as our grandfathers used.

Churchill: Talking about how you used up your sails. You know you said near the race's finish that you had one and a half spinnakers left. In the other race round the world I don't think there was so much sail damage?

Gill: Of course, we were sailing twice as far as in the last race. I think that most boats, particularly the big boats, in two legs of the last race would have had the same quota of damage.

Mullender: Yes, I'd agree. Chay Blyth arrived in Rio from Sydney with no mizzen and no spinnakers.

Churchill: What's the answer for other races – should you have stronger sailcloth?

Gill: I think a certain amount of technique could be improved.

Mullender: I did a survey of *G.B. II*'s sails yesterday. We have five busted spinnakers. They are all badly busted in a very similar way. Three of them have gone two feet up above the clew patch on one side and gone right across and up the opposite side as well. One – the storm spinnaker – could definitely be screwed down to defective workmanship. A starcut spinnaker has gone across the head . . .

Gill: That spinnaker has been once around the world already and doesn't owe us anything.

Mullender: It went at a reinforcing point on the luff tapes.

Churchill: Olivier?

de Kersauson: We always use too light a weight of cloth. And I asked my sailmaker to make me two very strong spinnakers. I want the mast to go, the boat to go, but with the spinnaker still flying. But in 35 knots one blew. I was very disappointed. The other did, too.

Gill: The thing I've learnt about racing, which is not new, is that starcut spinnakers are incredibly useful for running heavy, because you can flatten them down and keep the boat under control. But also, being a heavier sail, even in light airs when one would normally, in an inshore race, hoist the light sail, we hoist the heavy sail and hold it, so that even though the boat rolls, it does not tear. A light sail will tear itself to pieces.

de Kersauson: How many halyards did you break?

Gill: We didn't break any jib halyards but we broke one spinnaker halyard. We used to change over the spinnaker halyards at the top of the mast every day. It's a new type of limited stretch Marlow rope – it takes shock but doesn't give you too much drift when the wind blows. First thing in the morning, man up the mast, attach the other halyard, release the other. When it gets chafed, cut off a foot.

Churchill: And resplice?

Gill: No. We used bowlines to attach the halyard to the spinnaker and bowlines from sheet and guy.

Churchill: Olivier, how many halyards did you break?

de Kersauson: I broke one and then changed my system. I used wire. Then at the end of the wire I spliced a rope.

Gill: We had all wire halyards in our fore and aft sails but all the spinnaker gear was rope, including the guys. And instead of the sail being attached with a snapshackle to the guy, we had a rope loop attaching the guy to the clew of the sail, so that to release the guy we cut the rope loop every time. We would use a new rope with a reef knot in it every time.

Did you hoist your spinnaker in stops?

de Kersauson: I did not have any wool or rubber bands – we didn't buy them before the start – so I cut bands from garbage bags. Not working well but better than nothing.

Gill: We stopped too, in a 'star', half way down from the head and in from the clews. So we could pull the sail out to the pole before breaking.

Churchill: What is the longest day's run either of you have done?

Bagnall: 273 miles.

de Kersauson: 280 miles.

Gill: We were reported as doing more. On a day when we could not get a noon position and had to rely on D.R. [dead reckoning], and our log was reading badly, it seemed as if we'd done more.

Campbell: What are your feelings on this type of race?

de Kersauson: It is the most beautiful sailing you can make. I've been racing all over the world. I've raced the Hobart, Fastnet, in the United States, from L.A. to Hawaii, Tahiti: every race in the world. And after there'll be one missing – from Hong Kong or China back home.

Gill: We've enjoyed ourselves. For me it is the only form of racing. Obviously, I've taken part in other forms of racing but this is the most rewarding. To race this length of time and distance. Because it boils down to seamanship rather than money.

In a Channel race you can afford to forget the food, for example. In this race it is a fundamental principle that you must feed, and that morale must be high. You can do a Channel race without sleep but on a long race you must have sleep for the body to be efficient.

de Kersauson: It is the quality of the crew that matters because your crew is at sea for two months, and even if they are well trained they have not the same skill. On an ocean race, they've been in the office two days earlier. With this race, true seamanship appears.

Campbell: Did you really think you'd beat the clipper *Patriarch*'s record?

Gill: Looking at the figures in London, it looked difficult to beat, but suddenly we were both half way there with days in hand, so we took note.

A particular article in an English magazine stated that I and a services crew would never sail the boat properly and would never break the record, and it's given me great pleasure to disprove this.

9 Australia

The arrival of *Great Britain II* and *Kriter II* in Sydney on 7 November took the imagination and interest of Australians by storm. Not only had both yachts broken the record under sail from London but by arriving less than seven hours apart after a chase half way round the world they had allayed any fears about the value of a race between a mere four yachts. For several of the crew of both yachts it was a return to Sydney, where they had stopped on the Whitbread race. The yachts were berthed alongside an ammunition barge loaned by the Royal Australian Navy at the Royal Australian Naval Sailing Association clubhouse, a timeless place, but perhaps the most pleasant aspect of the return was seeing familiar faces once more.

Captain Jeff Gledhill, the very active and energetic commodore of the club, was, as ever, in full control of the administration of the welcoming reception and other familiar faces were among the crowd. Pedder Pedersen and his wife Teddy were standing by with the steaks that are so much part of Australian celebrations while Captain Max Hinchcliffe and Commander 'Woc' Roberts were on hand to offer advice about slipping the yachts for refit and the supply of stores and provisions.

For the crews concerned it was simply enough to be ashore, but the informal and yet sincere welcome certainly increased their appreciation. Initially the happiness of the French seemed a little overshadowed since they had to be content with second place, but the ice melted quickly and, very soon, as champagne, wine and beer flowed, all were celebrating together, not as crews of two separate yachts but as men who had shared a common struggle against forces far more powerful than themselves.

Mike Gill and his rival Olivier de Kersauson were soon surrounded by journalists and both gave spontaneous yet lucid replies to the hundreds of questions. Not least was the curiosity about the divergence of tactics in the southern Atlantic where *Great Britain II* had hugged the edge of the known high-pressure area and the French had steered the more westerly course recommended in the Ocean Pilot manuals. It was here, at the first conference, that any indication of a calculated gamble was

45. The morning after the night of the finish. *Great Britain II* berthed in Sydney, with the later arrival, *Kriter II*, beyond her

46. 'So that's how you did it.' Mike Gill, left, Yves Olivaux and French skipper Olivier de Kersauson compare tactics in Sydney

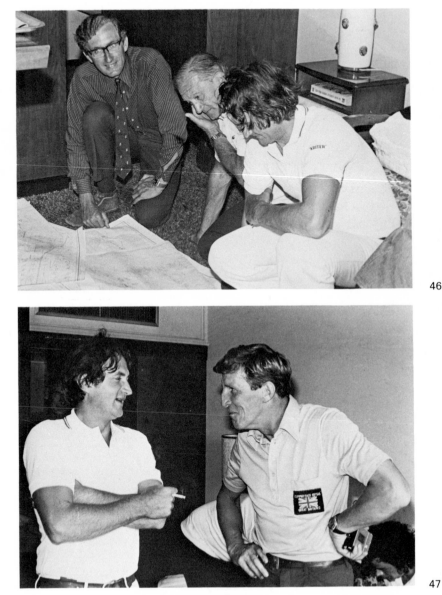

46

47

47. La psychologie . . . Olivier de Kersauson and Roy Mullender, start the battle of minds that lasted from Sydney to London

given and many people realized that below the apparently placid surface Mike Gill had as strong a personality as the forceful de Kersauson. The respect of the two men for one another, together with the rapport that built up between the French skipper and John Bagnall, was soon apparent.

While plans were put in hand to slip *Kriter II* ashore for repairs to the damage caused below the waterline by the whale, the two crews sailed in Sydney harbour aboard *Great Britain II*. While de Kersauson was at the helm, it was easy to see the interest and mental notes he made as he checked the readings of the instruments against the sail settings and performance of the yacht.

Receptions, invitations to Australian homes and parties followed in an endless round, but the highlight of the welcoming week was the barbecue party across Sydney harbour at a secluded spot just inside the towering North Head only accessible by boat – the Great Outdoors is part of Australia's way of life. Stores Beach, a perfect setting for a party, and reminiscent of a tropical beach in the Caribbean, became the target for the night and many small craft set out as dusk fell for an evening of complete relaxation where the seas of the Southern Ocean seemed a million miles and a thousand days away.

The celebrations over, temporarily, *Kriter* headed out to sea and up to Palm Beach, on Pittwater, an attractive stretch of water to the north of Sydney approached from the sea by Broken Bay. Here the yacht was slipped for repairs to the hull and for two weeks her crew were, for the main part, out of the social round of Sydney. *Great Britain II*, her crew for the return voyage to London now arriving in Sydney, sailed across the harbour to the Royal Australian Naval base in Balmoral Bay where she was also slipped for inspection and cleaning. Neither yacht showed signs of the distance sailed, apart from the obvious damage to *Kriter*. Weed and other underwater growth had little chance of survival in the cold southern seas, although the speed of the yachts might have had something to do with this, as was to be seen when the Dutch yacht *The Great Escape* was slipped a month later.

For the French crew there was more than just work to the hull and rigging facing them. Below decks chaos reigned, caused by condensation on the untreated bulkheads and deckheads.

The British yacht had few problems in this direction, although her new crew stripped the interior of the yacht bare and cleaned her right through with detergents and scrubbers. Her problem was sails, fourteen of which were either past repair or approaching the end of their useful life and since most of them had already been aboard for the previous circumnavigation this is hardly surprising. Storing was less of a problem as all stores were prepacked and those for the return voyage were already waiting aboard the Royal Fleet Auxiliary, *Tabartness*.

A certain amount of resentment became apparent between the crew of the French yacht and the British, a resentment that only flowed in one direction . . . from *Kriter*. Her crew, struggling to make repairs in a place that, while attractive to the tourist, was far from the yacht suppliers, felt that the British had an unfair advantage in the Naval base. The British, mainly ignoring the Gallic mutterings, politely pointed out that their only facility was a slipway and a jetty and that while the French were supported by a generous sponsor they themselves were short of funds. It was, in fact, obvious that the French were suffering, still, from the inordinate haste with which they had had to prepare their yacht for the original start of the race. Their frustration was not helped by observing the smooth and disciplined organization with which Mike Gill and, in Sydney, Roy Mullender, managed their crew.

Towards the end of November, just prior to the arrival of the Italian yacht *CS e RB II*, *Kriter II* returned to the Naval Sailing Association base at Rushcutters Bay and work began on the renovations below deck.

Olivier de Kersauson, meanwhile, began vociferous plans to enforce a delay of the restart from the planned date, 21 December, to the following week, 28 December. While he met with certain sympathy from some quarters he had to face the fact that the restart date had been decided for more than a year and only after considerable discussion between the race organizers and those who would be responsible for the start in Sydney. Apart from this the yachts competing in the annual Sydney to Hobart classic, as well as the Southern Cross Cup series, would be in Sydney at the nearby Cruising Yacht Club and their demands would, if a delay was permitted, place a considerable additional strain on the limited facilities.

The Italians, after a long struggle up the final stretch of coast from the Bass Strait, reached Sydney in the early hours of Sunday 30 November.

In a brilliant early sunlight they crossed the finishing line and were met by a small armada of craft which escorted them to the berth at the R.A.N.S.A. and the traditional steak breakfast. This greeting was double welcome as they had finished their food almost a fortnight earlier and had been limited to a cup of fresh water and a bowl of pasta per person each day since then. To prove the point a crew member aboard the yacht, Luigi Manzi, managed to eat seven steaks while the remainder of the team, including fashion model Elnora Waring, did almost as well.

The little Italian yacht, little compared with *Great Britain II* and *Kriter II*, had survived the 91-day passage well, although her stop at Recife had added almost 1,000 miles to her voyage. Her sails were in even more disastrous condition than those of *Great Britain II* and as money was short most of these were to be repaired by her crew and local sailmakers rather than replaced. They had obviously met worse weather conditions than the two leaders. Australian journalists were like bees around a honeypot when they discovered Elnora Waring but seemed to miss the significance in the story of a woman sailing around the world with seven men while practising yoga and vegetarianism; apart from a few over-posed pictures she escaped the grilling that was sure to await her on return to Britain from the more imaginative British, French and Italian press.

The successful first-leg crew of *Great Britain II* flew home leaving Dave Leslie as the only crew member, at this stage, to sail the complete distance around the world. The Royal Marine radio operator Keith Powell was later recalled to Australia to continue his impressive performance for the homeward leg and thus joined the exclusive band of yachtsmen who have rounded Cape Horn under sail in recent years.

As work progressed aboard the three yachts already in Sydney their crews were able to assess the Australian ketch *Anaconda II* at the Naval sailing centre. While *Anaconda*'s crew prepared themselves and their yacht for the race to Britain and while the electrical fittings and navigational equipment of the yacht impressed all who saw it, there was a certain amount of cynicism about her crew's apparent lack of sail training. The French crew regarded her mast and rig as generally too light for the seas ahead and others thought that total dependence upon electrically-cooked food from a deep freeze was a risk. Electrical equipment is the first to fail if life becomes difficult in the storms of the Roaring Forties and the northern Atlantic. While the yacht's crew pondered over the problems, her owner Josko Grubic sailed in the special race for maximum-sized yachts which was to precede the Southern Cross series and the Clipper Race. It was really little more than cocktail sailing and encouraged those who doubted that the yacht would start at all.

Meanwhile the French skipper had lobbied the Italian skipper, Doi Malingri, about delaying the start by one week and had tried, unsuccessfully, to persuade the new Dutch skipper, Dirk Nauta, to join the cause. Malingri was not against the idea but the taciturn Dutchman, whose yacht was still at sea, was adamant. He, his crew and his ship would start on 21 December even if they had less than a week to prepare. His main concern was to sail with a chance of reaching Cape Horn before the weather deteriorated and he knew there were two fresh crew members available ashore, and that the help of the local Dutch community and the assistance of the crew members leaving the yacht would make her ready in time.

Then to the chagrin of the French, Malingri announced that he was to put to sea alone in order to qualify for the single-handed transatlantic race to be sailed from Plymouth the following spring. To qualify he had to sail 600 miles alone and this he did, 300 miles straight out to sea and 300 miles back to Sydney, a lonely sojourn of four days, sailed on a convenient broad reach for the whole voyage in semi-tropical conditions – hardly the severe test that might have been preferred by the Atlantic race officials, but enough to qualify.

The festivities took on a more formal air as the start of the race approached and the Dutch yacht, *The Great Escape*, reached Sydney after 103 days at sea. Though this seemed slow compared with the leaders it compared favourably with the best time of *Cutty Sark* for the voyage and was very much in line with the average time of the Clipper ships, about 100–105 days for the outward passage. She arrived on 11 December after a frustrating crawl up the Australian eastern seaboard and looked as if she had simply sailed from Melbourne. Her decks showed little sign of wear and tear, though several sails needed renewing and several instruments, notably the electric impulse log, were unserviceable. The cause of this emerged when she was slipped for scrubbing at the near-by Cruising Yacht Club. Goose barnacles, native to the cold waters of the southern latitudes, had grown on every conceivable area of exposed metal hull including the toilet intakes, the log impeller mountings and

48, 49. The Australian *Anaconda II*, which joined the race for the second leg, shortly after launching in Adelaide. Some thought her rig too light for the Southern Ocean but she suffered damage only in the Tasman Sea between Australia and New Zealand

50. *The Great Escape* arriving in Sydney nearly five weeks after the
leaders and only ten days before the restart. In spite of this they were as
ready for sea again as the French crew of *Kriter II*.

the rudder bearings which, themselves, had worn. It was not considered a fault of the special anti-fouling paint, but of the way it had been rather hurriedly applied before sailing from Europe.

Ashore, the Sydney people had organized the Barbecue of the Year at Taraunga Park Zoo, attended by the Governor of New South Wales, Sir Roden Cutler, and Lady Cutler. Here the crew of *Kriter* received the City of Sydney prize for the first yacht in handicap to Australia and in his speech of thanks Olivier de Kersauson, dropping the formal address normal on these occasions and adopted by the other speakers, started his short address simply by saying 'Friends.' It more than summed up the spirit of the occasion as whole sides of beef roasted, alongside Tasmanian scallops and garlic prawns . . . all traditional Australian fare.

This splendid evening headed a week of receptions and followed the locally organized Maxi-Race for the yachts gathered in Sydney primarily for the annual race from Sydney to Hobart. Sponsored by City Ford, of Sydney, entry was limited to the largest ocean racing yachts; *Great Britain II*, *Anaconda II* and *Kriter II* were all eligible. *Great Britain* and *Anaconda* both appeared at the start, but *Kriter*, without steering hydraulics, stayed on her berth. The course, from within the confines of Sydney harbour to points out in the ocean, was visible from many vantage points along the coast ashore and thousands turned out to watch.

Of prime interest was the meeting between two vast American yachts, Jim Kilroy's *Kialoa* and Bob Johnson's *Windward Passage*. *Kialoa* was the latest conception in yacht design and construction, commissioned by her owner as the ultimate and regardless of expense. The older *Windward Passage* was designed by Alan Gurney, who was responsible for *Great Britain II*, though she had been built of wood and with less of an eye to economy. While *Windward Passage* was obviously more sophisticated in many ways than the British yacht the similarities were there; whenever they passed one another during sail training out in the Sydney harbour or beyond there was always a special cheer from each crew to the other. Others racing for the ostentatious City Ford Trophy included Jack Rooklyn's *Ballyhoo*, a large sloop designed by Bob Miller, patriotically painted in green and gold, the colours of Australia, and patriotically registered in Hong Kong! She was to sail against the veteran 12-metre yacht *Gretel*, which was looking her years, Rooklyn's first yacht *Apollo*, formerly a training yacht for Alan Bond's attempt to win the America's Cup, and the mighty New Zealand yacht *Buccanneer*.

It was obvious that the Clipper Race yachts would stand no chance against the stripped-out racing machines, particularly as they were both carrying full stores and water for a race of 13,000 miles, but the gesture of starting was enjoyed by the crews and appreciated by the spectators and the other contestants.

The race itself, over a course of thirty-five miles, was an absurdity for *Great Britain II* and *Anaconda II*. *Kialoa* and *Windward Passage* made flying starts pursued by *Ballyhoo*, which were the three main contenders, and *Buccanneer* while *Gretel* gave them an early fright. With the local sports minister steering *Great Britain* lost ground badly and *Anaconda II*, her decks covered with crew and spectators of every shape and size, arrived late at the starting line and brought up the rear.

Both yachts sailed the full course, *Great Britain* improving her performance in the hands of her regular helmsmen. To the chagrin of the Americans *Ballyhoo* won the cup. The race proved little except that *Great Britain* was a faster yacht than the 12-metre *Gretel*, and *Anaconda*, but the rivalry at the head of the fleet was replaced by a more leisurely attitude at the back.

Work aboard *Kriter* and *CS e RB II* continued right to the morning of the start from Sydney, the replacement hydraulics for *Kriter*'s steering gear arriving only two days before the departure date. All lobbying for a postponed start seemed to have ceased and most of the French crew had managed to spend at least a few days away from the yacht, many of them staying on homesteads well away from the sea. *Great Britain*'s crew had, of course, no need to leave, having joined for the second stage of the race although, again, one or two managed to escape for a day or two, one of them, Bill King-Harman, finding to his painful cost that riding horses in bare feet is bad for the ankles; he returned to the yacht with sores on his legs from stirrups that produced comments about the chain gangs of last century.

It seemed that *Kriter* would never be ready in spite of frantic efforts by her crew. The complete navigation area had been rebuilt, extra bunks added right aft in the driest cabin of the yacht and the whole accommodation area relined with condensation proofing, but the stores still littered the depths of the ammunition barge right up to the eve of sailing. Patrick Meulemeester had spent much time in the rigging checking every smallest fitting and it appeared that above deck all was well.

George Commarmond, acting as bosun, mate and cook, loaded his stores which still included a vast quantity of Chinese fish sauce. When ordering this in London he had expected to receive twenty-four 4- or 5-ounce bottles. In fact each bottle contained one litre, enough to keep a Chinese restaurant in business for years.

The comparison between the stores aboard the British and French yachts was interesting. The British were primarily supplied with pre-packed Army composite rations, each pack containing sufficient food for ten or five men for one day. The French had a less strict system of storing. Tins of camembert cheese, smoked oysters and other delights went aboard while the British had a quantity of specially-cured bacon from a curer in Yorkshire who had used the same recipe as had been used in Nelson's day. This bacon, when it arrived in Australia in November, had caused consternation among the Australian health officials who guard with special fervour against the possibility of any animal disease entering, quite justifiably given Australian dependence on meat and livestock products. The bacon was impounded in bond and then released just before departure.

On the eve of the restart the Royal Australian Naval Sailing Association gave one of its traditional farewell barbecue parties, steaks and champagne being made available in increasing abundance while the crews tried not to think of the morrow. Everyone who had endlessly manned the race control caravan, those who had worked in the bar and with the daily catering for the crews and many more besides were there. While the British and Dutch crews relaxed and enjoyed the festivities the Italians and the French were obviously less able to spend the last evening in complete abandonment, and de Kersauson kept his crew working for most of the night as there was an enormous amount of clearing-up to do before the morning.

The banter between the crews had been one of the amusing aspects of their stay in Sydney and Olivier de Kersauson was, without doubt, winner of any prizes that might have been awarded for the art of psychological warfare.

'Must I,' he asked, 'wait at Dover for *Great Britain II*, or may I sail straight on up the Thames and welcome Roy Mullender and his crew when they reach London?' This was typical of the man and next morning, as the crews joined their yachts for the start and he eased *Kriter* away from the barge to cheers from the British crew, he produced a beautifully timed aside: 'O.K. . . . Let's go to London, then.'

One of his crew, Patrick Meulemeester, was not to join the yacht for the return. Hit by one of the heaviest deck winches on the outward leg he had been lucky not to lose an arm and was obviously unhappy working on deck after this incident. During his stay in Australia he had worked almost unceasingly on the yacht, particularly on the masts, rigging and winches, which were his speciality; when the time came to leave he made the decision to stay behind which must have taken as much courage as deciding to sail. Gilles Varillon, a Frenchman sailing aboard *CS e RB II* during the first leg, had obviously made many friends among the crew of *Kriter* and was aboard the French yacht just before she slipped for sea. The skipper of *CS e RB II*, Doi Malingri, noticed this and shouted across,

'Gilles, are you coming with me or do you want to sail with them?'

'Can I stay?' replied the nervous Frenchman.

'Sure,' replied the Italian, 'just so long as I know.'

Varillon's kit was transferred and the Italians were down to seven crew, but the whole incident was more like the start of a race around the Sydney harbour than a race round Cape Horn to Europe.

For the Italians the start was like the lifting of a curtain. A week before they were due to sail the yacht had been inspected by the ubiquitous racing secretary of the Royal Ocean Racing Club, Alan Green. He had found that the liferaft had not been serviced as was prescribed by the race rules, and that there was no emergency radio aboard. He and the chairman of the race committee, John Roome, who had just been elected commodore of the R.O.R.C., decided, with the Australian Clipper Race committee, that this disqualified the Italians. The Italians promptly announced that they would sail anyway because they sailed for the pleasure of sailing and not to please committees. The disqualification was perhaps harsh and there were those in Sydney who felt that it was a little precipitate, but the Italian sponsors appeared to have run out of money or enthusiasm and there seemed no way that the crew of the yacht could acquire the £1,500 needed to put them back in the race. An article written after consultation with the Italians appeared in the *Financial Times* in London next morning and within twenty-four hours a London yachts-man, David Diehl, had telephoned to the *Financial Times* promising the necessary funds to help the Italians on their way. It was a completely unsolicited and spontaneous gesture and a sharp contrast to the reaction from local Italians in Sydney who had said that they would far rather help less fortunate Italian immigrants in Australia than those whose idea of a livelihood was to sail round the world in a yacht. Certainly a telephone conversation between one of the Italian crew in Sydney and a local Italian philanthropist sounded like an extract from *The Godfather*, but the real mystery was the lack of help from a sponsor who, until then, had never stinted with help when needed, but, in these times of recession, money had been the linchpin of the whole race.

10 Leave Cape Horn to Port

The day of the start from Sydney, 21 December, dawned bright and clear with a fresh wind blowing from the southeast. Although the race was not scheduled to begin until noon local time activity on the berths at the R.A.N.S.A. began hours earlier as the last preparations were put in hand. The waiting, the farewells and the light-hearted banter, often inconsequential, were all part of the last moments, moments that most of the crews would rather have missed for just putting to sea would ease the tension and would ease, too, facing the fact that the time to leave, the time that they had been working towards for weeks, had arrived.

The tension seemed greater ashore than aboard the yachts. For while those sailing had already come to terms with the task and the distance ahead, those ashore would be watching and waiting for news and the scale of the challenge really only dawned on them with the day of departure. Josko Grubic was as outwardly placid as anyone, saying his farewell to his wife, Renate, and his son and daughter as if he was simply returning to Adelaide. Roy Mullender was, as usual, quiet. Aboard *The Great Escape* Dirk Nauta and his team seemed totally relaxed. The crew of *Kriter* were still working, though, despite the time that they had been compelled to spend aboard, it was obvious that they had made many friends for life ashore. Captain Jeff Gledhill was marshalling the many spectators who wanted to sail to see the start and the Royal Australian Navy and Naval Reserve had provided extra craft to meet the demand.

Cheers echoed from crew to crew as they slipped mooring lines, bottles of rum were passed from *Great Britain II* to *Kriter II* and sparkling French wine was passed back to cries of 'See you in Dover' and replies of 'Never' or 'You'll be lucky.' *Great Britain II* flew a vast banner between her masts proclaiming 'Rule Britannia' and joined the hundreds of spectator craft heading for the starting line that stretched across the harbour, the same line that would be used a few days later for the start of the ocean race from Sydney to Hobart.

An hour before the start, with the Naval guard ship on station off Nielsen Park, south of the starting line, the police and Maritime Services

51. *Great Britain II* tacks for the open sea under the cliffs at the entrance to Sydney Harbour

53.   Minutes after the start *Great Britain II* leads the French
yacht *Kriter II* with the Italians aboard *CS e RB II* in
the foreground. The Australians aboard *Anaconda II* had passed
Great Britain II to leeward at the start and are out of the
picture to the left

52. *Great Britain II* and the Australian ketch *Anaconda II* wrestle for a good start as the gun fires to send them on their way from Sydney to Dover

54. *Anaconda II* powers her way through the vast spectator fleet to the entrance of Sydney Harbour and the open sea. *Great Britain II* is to windward astern and *Kriter II* further astern on the right

Board launches began marshalling the ever growing spectator fleet in an attempt to give the yachts a clear run for the line and on out to the Heads that guard the entrance of Sydney harbour. Thirty minutes before the start the five yachts began to test the wind strength at the line, *Anaconda* and *Great Britain* both making impressive runs at the line and then shying off back towards Sydney Harbour Bridge. *Kriter*, sailing for almost the first time since she reached Sydney, made a tentative swoop at the line and as the ten-minute preparatory gun fired from the Naval guard ship *Great Britain* and *Kriter* began their run for the line, a broad reach on starboard tack with *Anaconda* on their heels.

The British yacht was a few seconds early while the Australians had everything perfectly timed, hitting the line five seconds after the starting gun roared with the British on her heels and the French also in close attendance. The three yachts, with the Italians further down wind and a little astern, led the way out of Sydney harbour pursued by every type of pleasure craft from harbour ferries to canoes and sailing surfboards. Many of the spectator craft were deterred by the strong wind and heavy swell at the harbour entrance but a few of the larger yachts and power-boats ventured out to see *Great Britain* and *Kriter* both steal distance from the Australians as they tacked under the towering cliffs and set a course for the south of New Zealand. This was something of a problem as the winds were blowing from exactly the direction in which they wanted to steer. The wind kept in the southeast for almost two days, *Great Britain* and *Kriter* remaining separated by only a few miles until they met calm when they split tacks to try and hold the advantage off South Island, New Zealand.

Four days out from Sydney the winds backed to the northeast and freshened to 50 or 60 knots, hardly weather conducive to Christmas parties, but it was a long tough fast sail to the south and the Roaring Forties, exactly what each crew wanted as a Christmas present.

The wind moderated as dawn broke on Boxing Day, but only to about 40 knots. But it freed the leaders a little and *Kriter*, to leeward of *Great Britain* and sailing at almost her maximum speed, soon passed the British yacht through blinding spray and the icy winds that were giving surprised New Zealanders a white Christmas in their mid-summer. Spirits were high aboard *Kriter* as it seemed at last that they could make their yacht really move – and in sight of their rival.

Once clear of the British the French set about hardening sail as they came safely clear of the New Zealand mainland and the wind moderated a little more, but as they put the helm to windward nothing happened. They had been sailing, possibly for almost an hour, with no rudder but with the yacht perfectly balanced. Sheets were eased and she lay beam on to the sea as the sails were lowered and a single flare fired as *Great Britain II* approached. A quick inspection over the stern and in the steering locker aft confirmed the worst suspicions of the French. The rudder had gone. Seas were too high to risk passing lines from one yacht to another, but while the French assessed the situation *Great Britain II* stood by until Olivier de Kersauson, his heart heavy with disappointment, waved Roy Mullender and his crew on their way with cries of '*Bon voyage*.' He inched their yacht round to the north, head to wind, while ways of steering her were devised.

A radio call was sent to Sydney that the rudder was lost but that there was no damage. The yacht would back to Sydney as best she could under jury steering gear. Thoughts of sailing for New Zealand, much closer than Australia, 900 miles away, were abandoned as it was considered unlikely that a new rudder could be built quickly there, or that there was a slip available that could accommodate the yacht. It was Boxing Day and a double irony for de Kersauson: in the Tasman Sea two years earlier, on 30 December, he had been aboard Eric Tabarly's *Pen Duick VI* when she had been dismasted. *Great Britain II*, her crew as disappointed as the French by their departure from the fray, headed on to the southeast and the winds of the Southern Ocean. The French, with a spinnaker pole fitted with sheets of alloy as a sweep rudder, began to inch their way home, but the final stab of fate was still to hit them. Three or four hours after turning back and while making tracks for Sydney, they saw their rudder, a white wedge of aluminium aerofoil, floating in the sea less than 100 yards from the yacht, but without steering gear, indeed without that very rudder, they were unable to do more than watch it float away towards the Antarctic and Cape Horn.

Ashore in Sydney all was relatively peaceful, the race to Hobart had started with a record entry of 102 yachts and a listening watch was being kept for *Kriter*. Those waiting for her estimated that she would reach Sydney, at best, on 4 or 5 January and this opinion was endorsed by the navigating officer of H.M.S. *Glamorgan*, a Royal Naval ship that headed a flotilla visiting Australian and Far Eastern waters and was at that time in Hobart, Tasmania.

56

57

55, 56, 57. The crew of *Great Britain II* unhappily watches *Kriter II* shortly after the French had lost their rudder while passing actually in sight of the British yacht south of New Zealand. The French rode out the rough seas with a single headsail while they inspected the damage, and then sailed slowly back to Sydney, 600 miles to the north-east, with a jury rudder

The panic that was soon created emanated from ill-informed and sensation-seeking French journalists who, in Sydney and France, insisted that thirteen gallant Frenchmen were lost in the ferocious Tasman Sea. Pressure was put on the local French consular office from relatives and a search was demanded. Life aboard *Kriter* however was relatively peaceful as she headed northwest at about 100 miles per day, balancing head sails and mainsail with a mizzen staysail that was hoisted and lowered as needed. The reason for the lack of communication had been discovered by Julian Gildersleeve when he removed the radio aerial connection between the main radio and the triatic stay and found it flooded with sea water, thus leaving him with the emergency set, with a range of about 150 miles and powered by crank handle, to communicate with the rest of the world.

Aboard H.M.S. *Glamorgan* in Hobart, Captain Robert Leathes knew that his ship, and H.M.S. *Berwick* which was sailing with her, were the only two Naval vessels on the eastern seaboard of the Australian continent capable of putting to sea at relatively short notice, Christmas leave being the Australian Naval order of the day. Under increasing pressure from the French and now supported by some of the Clipper Race committee, an aircraft of the Australian Air Force was instructed to make a search. It took a direct course from Sydney to the southeast towards southern New Zealand, picked up faint morse signals and then sighted the yacht 200 miles from Sydney rolling her way peacefully northwestwards. For some elements of the French press it had become a moment of anti-climax, but for almost everyone else a time of relief and two days later a party of French residents chartered a local fishing-boat, *Aquarius*, from game fisherman Bidge Holmes and sailed out to meet her.

The search party sailed southeastwards for five hours at about 9 knots and then turned north. Just as the sun was dropping over the Australian coast they saw the yacht, still 9 miles away towards the north, and as dusk fell a tow line was passed and the long haul back to Sydney began. It was typical of Australians that even though the yacht returned to the Naval centre at 2 a.m. on 4 January, there was a crowd of friends to greet her. There could be no celebrations but a brave attempt was made by the disappointed crew to put a bold face on the matter and a lot of help was given by those ashore to ease the sadness.

Once *Kriter II* left the race, some of the fire that had been so much part of the first leg seemed to have disappeared but no sooner had Olivier de Kersauson reached Sydney he, to the surprise of some of those ashore, announced that he was still in the race and required immediate facilities to slip his yacht and make a new rudder. Both requests presented a problem for it had already been decided that the slipway at the Cruising Yacht Club was unsuitable for the yacht, its state of repair leaving much to be desired, and even if Palm Beach, the original slipping place after the yacht's arrival, could take the task on, there were problems with the tides.

Money, it seemed, was not a problem but, in spite of the diligence of Captain Max Hinchcliffe, a slipway was. He tried the Naval authorities and the Harbour Board but there were no berths available until Vickers (Australia) Ltd, with a shipyard above the Harbour Bridge, said they could slip the yacht while Halvorsen's Shipyard were prepared to remake a rudder and the support needed for the skeg. It seemed that the loss of the rudder was due to alterations made by the French themselves when the yacht was slipped in Lymington before the start; they had added a counter-balance to the foot of the rudder, protruding ahead of the rudder and rudder shaft and fitting flush to the bottom of the keel. Some timber, rope or other flotsam had become trapped between this protrusion and the keel and when hydraulic pressure was applied the rudder was unable to pivot on the mountings. Something had to give way, and it was the special alloy mounting at the foot of the rudder shaft. Once this had broken the rudder was merely supported by the fittings at the top of the shaft. A few good seas on the flaying plate and it broke free.

Both the smaller yachts had had their problems in the rough weather. *CS e RB II* was knocked down and virtually capsized, but she was well battened down at the time and her helmsman was in the steering position below decks using the bubble dome. *The Great Escape* had been sailing within fifty yards of the Italians for a considerable time during the days between Christmas and New Year, when *Kriter* and *Great Britain* were so close together ahead; her crewman Jan Carree was badly injured after being swept to the deck in heavy seas. He suffered cuts to his head and legs which were stitched by Jose Detmers, a nurse sailing as one of the crew. Confined to his bunk for several days, he was reported to be well and comfortable by skipper Dirk Nauta.

During this time *Great Britain II* was continuing a fast passage eastwards towards Cape Horn, heading for the 60th latitude south with

58, 59. *Kriter*'s jury rudder, made of a spar and aluminium
sheeting, with which she limped back to Sydney

58

59

60. *Right* The new rudder built and fitted to *Kriter II* at Vickers
(Australia) shipyard. It was thought that her original rudder
was lost when weed or debris stuck between the rudder and
the counterbalance ahead of it

Anaconda making even more southing to attempt the shortest Great Circle route to Cape Horn and to avoid headwinds that had been met in the Fifties. Off the south of New Zealand all the yachts had met heavy weather, alternating with the calms that had slowed *Kriter*'s return to Sydney.

Josko Grubic and *Anaconda* had closed the oil rig that lies in the Foveaux Strait, between the southern mainland of New Zealand and off-lying islands. Here the Australians repaired broken rigging and checked their masts and spars for further damage. In a conversation with the oil rig operators, they described how they had closed the western New Zealand coast and needed special charts for their computerized OMEGA navigation system, but other than this, and some rigging problems, all was well. The charts were sent by air to New Zealand and then dropped from a light aircraft chartered from a local flying club while the yacht was off Bluff. They then proceeded on their way, an estimated 500 miles astern of the British yacht, but with the smaller Italian and Dutch yachts very much on their heels.

Once in the Southern Ocean and south of the 57 degree latitude of Cape Horn the yachts encountered increasing headwinds, as they were already south of the latitude of the notorious Roaring Forties.

From the reports received in London via Sydney radio it seemed that the southerly route, down to 60 degrees and more to the south, was considered the tactically correct course although two years earlier only the Naval yacht *Adventure*, with Roy Mullender aboard as mate, and the first *CS e RB* had bettered this. Now it was like a main road.

Great Britain led the way to the Horn, averaging better than 200 miles each day and making time on *Anaconda II* astern whose crew radioed reports of headwinds and calms. Later they reported reaching 66 degrees south, almost the Antarctic Circle, seeking a way past Cape Horn.

In Sydney work aboard *Kriter* progressed well and although there were delays in airfreighting further hydraulic parts she was soon ready for sea once more. She restarted from the same starting line on 18 January at 11 a.m. local time in such haste that the race officials scarcely had time to lay the starting-line marks. Once more the Sydney sailors turned out in strength to see her go and once more the sword-rattling words of Olivier de Kersauson, sprinkled with the customary humour, left their mark.

'Tell that Mullender that I have broken 200 metres of masts in the last few years at sea. I wish 'im and 'is crew no problems, but there are still many miles to go and when *Kriter* approaches the Channel they will think at 'eathrow it is Concorde coming from Rio I will be going so fast. I only hope I can stop O.K. at Dover to shake Roy by the hand and take 'is record from 'im.'

It was obvious that the French were back in the chase with a vengeance. Even if they could not make up the four weeks that they had lost, they were determined to better any time returned by the other yachts and to establish, if not a new record against *Patriarch*'s time, certainly the fastest time under sail from Sydney to London in this century. The Royal Ocean Racing Club in London, meanwhile, had announced that there would be no penalty for the assistance the French had received from the fishing-boat *Aquarius*, an announcement that brought shrieks of laughter from the French – another indication that while yachtsmen who sail around the world respect rules and enjoy the organization that gives status and coordination to the event, their primary interest is sailing and that has priority over any committee.

When *Kriter* restarted from Sydney *Great Britain* was already rounding Cape Horn and *Anaconda* was well south of the Horn heading for the turn. *The Great Escape* and *CS e RB II* were still battling through the Southern Ocean more than 1,000 miles behind the Australians; the Dutch were leading the Italians, but there appeared to be discrepancies in the positions reported by Doi Malingri and his crew which bore little relationship to those of the apparently slower Dutchmen.

These discrepancies were to be shown up clearly later in the month once the Italians had rounded Cape Horn and had established radio contact with the *Bransfield*.

The radio operators aboard the British survey ship *Bransfield*, which was en route for the British Antarctic Base at Hailey Bay, had been doing some fine work, far beyond the normal call of duty of their already arduous and demanding life. Hugh O'Gorman, the first operator to contact any of the yachts, first heard *Great Britain* while *Bransfield* was still heading south; then he managed to make contact with *Anaconda*, with *The Great Escape* and finally with *CS e RB II*. While holding generally social conversations with the crews he also took their positions and passed them back to Cambridge where the survey operations have their base.

61

62

63

61, 62, 63.   Freezing fog, gale force winds and spray. Life in
the depths of the Southern Ocean was far from pleasant for
any of the crews. These conditions lasted for almost a week
as the yachts sailed as far as 60 degrees south, into iceberg-
infested waters

64. *Great Britain II* running in fine weather but still steep
seas in the Southern Ocean

These positions were in turn passed to the *Financial Times* and onwards to interested people in Australia, Italy and Holland. It was hard to establish why the Italian skipper, Doi Malingri, was giving positions that were at least 24 hours old until he reported to Mr O'Gorman that they had lost a spreader, a support strut on the mast, and were already at Cape Horn heading for Stanley, in the Falkland Islands, to repair rigging and their main radio, which once more had failed.

The radio officer, though obviously a kindly man, told the Italian in no uncertain terms what he thought of the falsified positions. It might have been, after all, the survey-ship crews who had to search if anything had failed aboard the yachts and, if, off Cape Horn, or to the west of it, the last reported position had been 150 to 200 miles wrong, then the expensive search would have been entirely futile. This rap on the knuckles was repeated to the Italian crew when they stopped at the Falkland Islands by an officer of the British Antarctic Survey.

Reporting false positions had occurred in the first leg of the race and in other races over great distances, but never when matters of safety and survival were concerned.

The gallant Dutch aboard *The Great Escape*, in spite of a buffeting in the Southern Ocean that had occasional respites of calm and the risk of collision with icebergs, rounded Cape Horn ahead of the Italians.

As the British crew rounded the Horn on 16 January, 26 days out of Sydney, the French were making final preparations for their restart. Once on their way they were to average a pace that made those ashore feel that the time set by *Great Britain* for the second leg of the race would, if a new record, only be held for as long as *Kriter* was at sea.

Great Britain, once past the Horn, began heading north for the Falkland Islands, breaking clear of the easterly winds that had dogged her as she headed for the notorious Cape.

These wind were causing similar problems for the Australians aboard *Anaconda*. They were three days behind and had reported to the survey ship that they had sailed so far south in an attempt to dodge the unexpected calms and headwinds. Olivier de Kersauson had never seemed impressed by the reputation of Cape Horn and merely regarded it as a point to be passed. But even though it failed to produce the weather

7. The greys and greens of the ocean. *Anaconda II* battling
   through a storm in a welter of spray and misty sunlight

8. *Great Britain II* surfing under reduced sail in the Southern Ocean, David Leslie at the helm and big seas building astern in spite of the indicated speed of 15 knots and more

9. One of the many small, but dangerous icebergs seen in the Southern Ocean from *Great Britain II*
10, 11. Running and rolling down wind aboard *Great Britain II* in the fresh winds of the south-east Trades

9

10

12.   The final moment of triumph. On a brilliant spring
day *Great Britain II* sails under spinnaker through
Tower Bridge into the Pool of London

which has given it its fearsome reputation, rounding it was certainly good for the morale of the crews.

As yachts approached the Horn they found difficulty in reporting their positions, probably because radio signals to Europe were blocked by the South American continent while Australia and New Zealand were by this time too far astern to pick up the transmissions. The help from *Bransfield* did much to overcome the difficulty; she kept in touch with the yachts and for a considerable time after they had turned northwards from the Horn for home. When the *Bransfield* eventually went to the extreme south, to Halley Bay in Coat's Land, the listening and relaying of signals was taken over by the British survey base at Sydney Island.

Once into the South Atlantic navigators could leave the Falkland Islands to port or to starboard. The British crew passed them to the east and the Australians, who had rounded the Horn on 19 January, 29 days out of Sydney, went the other side. The doubtful wisdom of this was demonstrated a little later when *Anaconda* was slowed appreciably while *Great Britain* romped her way northwards in winds of 50 knots from the southeast; after she had covered 1,500 miles in the first week after rounding the Horn the wind moderated to 35 knots, or a full gale.

The British yacht, with her crew of sixteen servicemen, temporarily strengthened military presence in the South Atlantic. A company of Royal Marines were based in the Falkland Islands at the time and the addition of the British yacht crew to the South Atlantic briefly increased this presence by fifty percent. Rule Britannia!

Next to pass Cape Horn, on 26 January, only seven days behind *Anaconda*, was *The Great Escape* whose crew appeared to be having a much happier time of it that those who had sailed her to Australia in the first half of the race. There was now no news of *CS e RB II*, but she finally appeared at Stanley, the capital town and port of the Falkland Islands. Ahead *Great Britain* was passing out of latitude 30 south and her crew celebrated with a party, opening special food packs reserved for such occasions. Bill Porter surprised the crew by attending the party in a mini-skirt. Obviously it was time to hurry on home!

As they headed north to the equator they met the beginnings of the lighter winds in the equatorial waters while *Anaconda* was chasing them once more in the fresh winds that the British had now left behind. The

65. Owen Trewatha, a watch leader aboard *Anaconda II*, at the helm in
the Southern Ocean

66. Sailing down a main road? The stern wash of *Anaconda II* as she
reached her maximum speed surfing in the Southern Atlantic at
almost 20 knots

Australians stayed near the South American coast in spite of warnings in the navigation manuals that winds are less reliable inshore than out in the ocean where the southeasterly tradewinds can almost be guaranteed.

CS e RB II remained in Stanley for the first few days of February while *The Great Escape* headed northeast in the track of *Great Britain*; if, as some felt, the Dutch had held the handicap lead at Cape Horn, she was losing this as they headed home.

Anaconda's choice of the more coastal route by the South American seaboard, now appreciated by both the owner and his navigator to be the less prudent choice, became a necessity as the yacht passed the latitude of Buenos Aires in fearsome seas and strong winds. Here the yacht suffered a 'knockdown' as she came off a wave that met all the requirements of size and ferocity to earn the designation 'freak'. The yacht rolled over away from the wind, her mast and rigging burying in the water, and there was immediate chaos above and below decks. Fortunately the damage was less severe than that suffered by the Mexican yacht *Sayula* two years previously when the same trouble occurred in the Southern Ocean during the Whitbread race. *Sayula*, eventual winner of the Whitbread race, was a standard production Swan 65, designed by Sparkman and Stephens and built in Finland. While sailing in heavy seas at 47 degrees south she fell from the front of a following wave of immense proportions, her mast falling outwards down into the trough ahead of the wave away from the wind as the yacht slewed sideways. The wave then broke over the yacht virtually capsizing her. On deck several of the crew found themselves in the rigging while below decks batteries and stores rained from below the cabin floor, bursting on the cabin ceilings and causing considerable havoc and several injuries to crew. It was several days before life was restored to normal both above and below decks. *Anaconda*, with her comparatively slight damage, was lucky.

Two of the crew, including the yacht's doctor, Douglas Justins, were injured below decks and while their injuries seemed serious, their actual extent was not easy to diagnose. Once the yacht was 'on her feet' and sailing again it was decided to head towards Rio de Janeiro, where the injured could be put ashore for treatment, if they had not recovered. The ground made on *Great Britain* was soon lost again. When a mere 100 miles south of the Brazilian port, it was decided to go on with the injured men and a hitch was taken out to the east to round the mass of the eastern Brazilian seaboard and the course was reset for the North Atlantic.

Doug Justins had also realized, along with the remainder of the *Anaconda*'s crew, that their skipper was not as fit as he himself had believed or had led them to believe; he was still troubled by the injuries arising from the accident which occurred prior to the launching almost a year earlier. Long periods of standing in the lurching and pitching boat were more than he could take in spite of his obvious determination, and it was necessary to prescribe longer periods of rest.

While *Anaconda* was solving her problems off Brazil, *Great Britain* was more than 10 degrees further north, well out into the Atlantic and still making good progress northwards. The Italians were still at Stanley in the Falklands and the Dutch were now well north of the Falklands making a steady 160 miles a day in the south Atlantic trades.

The race seemed at risk of becoming processional, but this fear vanished when the reports came through from the French aboard *Kriter*. They were now 15 days out from Sydney and already estimating their rounding of Cape Horn to be a mere week away, thus bettering the time of the British yacht by an astonishing 5 days. The British time of 26 days from Sydney to Cape Horn had seemed remarkable enough, equalling that taken by the yacht on the earlier Whitbread race. Even though the French had less trouble with unexpected and unpredictable headwinds in the Southern Ocean than the yachts which had preceded her, the effort was impressive and will probably stand for many years as an unofficial record for yachts limited in size by the International Offshore Rule. Having rounded Cape Horn with 5 days in hand over the time of the British, *Kriter* maintained a fast average speed into the Southern Atlantic, taking a course east of that sailed by both the British and Dutch crews. But *Great Britain* had slipped through the feared Doldrums, to the north of the equator, with only one and a half days of light frustrating winds before finding the beginnings of the northeast trades some 600 miles south of the Cape Verde Islands.

Here, with the stars of the northern latitudes now showing clearly in the sky and the final stages of the race beginning to act as a carrot to the weary crew, a lighter moment of the race occurred for both those taking part and those at home. When sending their reports to Britain, the crew of *Great Britain* had been sending a weather situation, usually via the Army Apprentices School at Harrogate, indicating the wind force and direction relative to the course and speed of the yacht. While still in the southeast trades, just south of the equator, Roy Mullender had sent a report that indicated that he was sailing in a southeasterly wind on a course almost true north with the wind ahead of the yacht. Wanting to give *Financial Times* readers accurate details, I politely queried this, and deservedly received the following reply:

In reply to signal 'South East Trades',
Who is this journalistic clown
That questions what I've written down?
In this scientific age
We measure speed by wind and speed by gauge
We care about the wind we feel
And subtle points of trim and heel.
Now, if you study books and charts
You'll find that wind in these here parts
Is known to blow from east to west,
Though south east true is commonest.
If confusion has occurred
'Tis not through misuse of word.
These Trades which mark the route for barques
Were named by salts and not by clerks.

**The opportunity was too tempting to miss and this reply was sent to
Great Britain II:**

When heading north on starboard tack,
You must have almost been aback
In spite of talk of southeast trade
And courses for fair England made.
But then with such a motley crew
Of soldiers some and airmen few
It really made it so much worse
The Navy, starting writing verse.
Navigation you may know,
But when you signal, kindly show
The way the wind is felt to blow
So desk-bound clerks can help you solve
The route for home and those you love.

Once through the Doldrums and making a good heading towards the Azores, 57 days out from Sydney and well within sight of the new record for the voyage from Australia and therefore the full circumnavigation,

67.   Rolling home under reduced, but well balanced sail. A reefed mainsail, a small headsail boomed
out to the opposite side of the yacht, and steep grey seas in the approaches to the north Atlantic

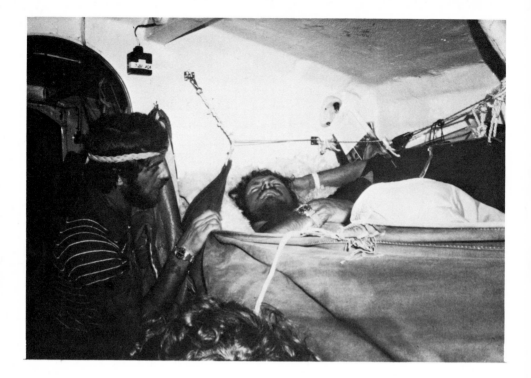

68. Sleep was a welcome alternative to the rough, cold
conditions on deck. Bob Bell gets his share

the British yacht fell into the calms that are the dread of every sailor, especially those trying to race the clock. On 16 February, about 600 miles south of the Azores, the winds fell light and Roy Mullender reported that they had covered only 80 miles during the previous day, but the north Atlantic weather chart was holding more promise and the next day the wind filled from the northwest and they were back to an encouraging 10 knots through reasonable seas and a direct course for home.

Kriter meanwhile, 34 days out from Sydney, was now between 3 and 4 days ahead of *Great Britain*'s time to latitude 35 south, off Buenos Aires, and still making impressive speed in the southeast trades. *Anaconda* was free of the Doldrums, 1,400 miles astern of *Great Britain*, and *The Great Escape* was approaching them still maintaining her 160 miles per day and the exact course taken by the British yacht.

Before running into the calm weather south of the Azores, *Great Britain* had problems with her steering gear, which failed while sailing in fresh winds, but the crew on deck were quick to rig the emergency tiller and steered with this while the broken steering wires from wheel to rudder-head were repaired. It all sounded easy, but this itself was a sure sign of the skill and professionalism of the crew. They were thankful, once through the latitude of the Azores, that the problem had manifested itself when it did and not a few days later.

Once west of the Azores the wind freshened and backed to the southwest, and the yacht was about to be given the kick she needed to stay in touch with the 69-day Clipper record. Steering about 050 degrees magnetic, the direct course for Ushant, the most northwesterly point on the Brittany coast, she surged her way northeast at speeds of 15 knots and more. Broken steering gear here would have been a frightening and dangerous business, but everything held together and the finishing line, now only 1,000 miles away, was approaching at a steady 11 knots. As one of the crew said later, in Dover, 'It was a great feeling to go down after an exhilarating four hour watch to know that when one came up again eight hours later we were 100 miles nearer home.'

Meanwhile Roy Mullender, speaking to his wife Jean by radio, estimated that they would reach Dover within 5 days, on Thursday 26 February, 3 days inside the 69-day record of the *Patriarch*.

The spotlight now focused on the British yacht as she wound off the final miles at a steady average of 250 miles a day. She reported surges at surfing speeds of almost 20 knots, 6 knots faster than her maximum designed hull speed, as she roared into the Bay of Biscay, still riding the southwesterly gale. For her crew it was an anxious and yet exciting time. Home was nearly in sight but they knew that the yacht was finishing her second circumnavigation and that in sailing from Sydney to Dover they shared only a quarter of the strains the yacht had taken over her 50,000 miles of sailing through the toughest waters of the world.

On the morning of 23 February, 3 days inside the estimated finishing date set by her crew, the yacht was 250 miles west-southwest of Ushant, still maintaining her fast pace and the next morning was off the north-west French headland sailing at 10 knots and more through thick mist into one of the busiest shipping lanes in the world. Even her crew, who by now were hardened to anything that the weather could throw at them, admitted that they were worried by sailing through heavy shipping in almost no visibility. The look-outs who had been posted in the Southern Ocean to watch for the icebergs were now forward once more listening for the foghorns of ships and the churning of engines, a sound that carries as well as a foghorn across water.

Once round Ushant they met the first of the Channel tides running against them. The course was set to pass north of the Channel Islands but to hold the southern side of the Channel to avoid the lighter weather forecast for the English coast. Watch-keeping fell by the wayside as the Channel Islands were passed, and the tide race off Alderney was the next problem. It was fair once more and the decreasing west wind left the slowing yacht open to the danger of being pushed down the tide-race towards Guernsey. This they avoided, but the next six hours of darkness, into the dawn of 26 February, saw little easterly progress as they stemmed the tide and inched northeast across the Channel before picking up the flood once more which carried them, under spinnaker, mainsail, mizzen staysail and mizzen, along the Sussex coast towards Dover.

Meanwhile the banker and philanthropist, Jack Hayward, who had originally sponsored the building of *Great Britain II* for Chay Blyth, had his enthusiasm for yachting rekindled when reports of its new success reached him. He had given Chay the yacht following his line honours success in the Whitbread race two years earlier and had then sponsored the building of the maximum-sized trimaran, *Great Britain III*, for the

1975 Whitbread multihull Atlantic triangle. This race was cancelled leaving Chay and his sponsor with a vast yacht and nowhere to go. Now his unhappiness was forgotten and as soon as he heard that *Great Britain II* and her new crew were about to make yachting history, Jack Hayward was busy flying from his Bahamas home to Britain to greet the crew.

While *Great Britain II* faced one final bout of contrary tide off the Sussex coast, the crowds gathered at Dover. Meanwhile, the Royal Cinque Ports Yacht Club members who were hosts for the finish braced themselves for a daytime arrival. This was not to be, though photographs of the final day at sea were already to hand ashore from several expeditions made by light aircraft and the crews of R.A.F. Strike Command in Nimrod aircraft from St Mawgan in Cornwall. The R.N.R. minesweeper *Isis*, crewed by the Southampton University division of the reserve, accompanied *Great Britain II* past the final headland off Folkestone and the Dover lifeboat escorted her into Dover. At 11.32 p.m. G.M.T. she crossed the finishing line to the firing of maroons and the bellows of the Dover harbour entrance foghorn, but the real welcome, the one the crew had been waiting for, was ashore, where hundreds, unable to go afloat, waited on the jetty where the yacht would berth. It was over. The 69-day record had been broken by more than 2 days in a time of 66 days, 22 hours, 31 minutes and 35 seconds.

The celebrations, thanks to the kindness of the yacht club, local magistrates and others, continued until dawn, and stopped only then because, while the energy of the yachtsmen seemed boundless, those ashore were certainly seeming to flag a little. The engineer of the lifeboat played the spoons until his hands must have ached, accompanying one of the local officers of H.M. Customs, whose expertise on the guitar seemed to increase with the lateness of the hour.

Next morning the full impact of their arrival began to become a reality to the crew. Reactions were varied but the common realization was that the target had been achieved, that the yacht was firmly tied to a sheltered berth inside the inner harbour at Dover with nothing more to be achieved. There were no more watches to keep, no more struggles with flogging sails, no more long hours trying to make radio contact or waiting for the sun and stars to break through to give an accurate position. In the place of these labours were the realities of everyday life. Bank statements, bills, mortgages and road fund licences.

69

70

69,70.   Not even the cold of a February night could deter those welcoming *Great Britain II* to Dover. Above, Roy Mullender attacks the champagne with his wife Jean, left, while John Langthorne, against the mast, talks to Australian Julia Steele who was responsible for many of the arrangements in Australia and who was at Dover for the arrival, well protected from the English winter. Below, the celebrations continue. The Dover lifeboat which escorted *Great Britain II* into the harbour is alongside. All the other yachts received a similar greeting regardless of the time of day or night

71. Fifteen happy men in Dover on the morning after the finish, with Nelson, the *Great Britain*'s mascot at the helm. The Royal Marine radio operator, Keith Powell, to the right of the mast with David Leslie, the mate, who sailed the full distance

The return from a small hard world shared with fifteen other men to the world of civilization made them wonder whether it was really civilized.

The question, which was heard more and more as the first day in port passed, was where were the French. Another problem that was beginning to worry the race committee was the position of the Italians aboard *CS e RB II*; they had left Port Stanley three weeks earlier and since then had not been sighted nor made radio contact. *Anaconda* had made direct radio contact with Britain several days before *Great Britain* finished from a position well south of the Azores; Josko Grubic sounded despondent that they were continually beset by headwinds, claiming only 6 days of fair winds since leaving Sydney, though the roots of his apparent despondency were shown later to be deeper than the weather. The Dutch, as reliable as ever on their radio, were on the equator as *Great Britain* finished. The colourful and ever-gallant Olivier de Kersauson made both his presence at sea and his threat to the newly established record felt in Dover; when Jean Mullender, wife of the skipper of *Great Britain*, went to her hotel room in Dover, she found three dozen of the finest pink roses awaiting her sent from de Kersauson via his radio and Interflora with his profoundest respects. At the time he was still 3 days ahead of the time taken to the latitude 10 degrees south by *Great Britain*, but was to lose a day in the Doldrums.

While the British crew cleaned their yacht and became accustomed once more to beds that did not move in the night, and to nights that were not divided into watches of four hours, *Anaconda* made her way past the Azores; but when the British sailed for a triumphal welcome in London she was only on the latitude of Cape Finisterre, northwest of Spain and some 250 miles out into the Atlantic. As if to repeat the headwinds that had beset them in the southern hemisphere, the Australians entered the Western Approaches in a weather pattern that had all the makings of easterly winds, and as they entered the Channel for the final three hundred miles to Dover, the high pressure over the Scandanavian countries pushed air towards the low pressure in the Atlantic and *Anaconda* had to beat the final miles to the finish against a headwind.

A touching and appropriate moment at Dover was the presentation of a small specially-prepared bale of wool to the Deputy Constable of Dover Castle from the Constable, the former Australian premier Sir Robert Menzies. The wool had been carried aboard *Great Britain* from Sydney and was a reminder of the days when wool had been the principal cargo of clippers sailing from Australia to Britain; indeed it had been the cargo of *Patriarch* during her maiden record-breaking homeward voyage.

Once more relatives and friends converged on Dover which the crew of *Anaconda* expected to reach on Sunday. But this was not to be and those waiting watched the flag on Dover Castle stream westwards, sharing the struggle of the crew as they knew it gave them a fresh headwind. Eventually, they too reached Dover, on 8 March at 11.07 p.m., 78 days and a few hours from Sydney. For a crew who had gained little experience of their yacht before the start, and who had not had the opportunity offered by the first leg of the race to build a team and learn each other's foibles, the crew of *Anaconda* had achieved a success of their own. They had lost their power supply, and there was no lighting aboard the yacht. Their deep-frozen food had been lost with the power supply and they had managed to make the packs of composite rations, given to them by the British in Sydney when *Great Britain* was restocked for the second leg, last for a month – a quantity of food intended to feed a crew of thirteen for about two weeks. There had been those in Australia, knowledgeable yachtsmen among them, who thought that the rig of *Anaconda* was too light for the task ahead and the accommodation too luxurious, but the facts to the contrary were evident when the yacht reached Dover.

The rigging of *Anaconda* had stood up to the worst weather in the Southern Ocean and the Atlantic; her crew attributed most of her problems off southern New Zealand to lack of testing and preparation rather than design faults. On arrival at Dover the accommodation below decks was still of Hilton standards when compared to the spartan and entirely practical accommodation of *Great Britain* and the basic survival conditions aboard *Kriter*.

In spite of the late hour, Dover once more stretched itself far beyond the bounds of normal hospitality and the fact that *Anaconda* had finished second was not reflected in the celebration. It was as fine a welcome as that afforded *Great Britain* and many of the British crews of both legs had travelled to Dover to greet the Australians. *Great Britain*, meanwhile, had sailed to the Thames where she had moored for a night at Greenwich and then, steered by Edward Heath, with spinnaker set and Tower Bridge specially raised, she berthed above Tower Bridge for a special welcome at Tower Pier. Hundreds of Londoners came to the river to greet her and she then completed the full circuit by entering St Katherine's Haven, just below Tower Bridge, where she was open to the public. Meanwhile the anxious eyes of all her crew were still watching the progress of *Kriter* as she threateningly reeled off the final miles and maintained her lead of almost 3 days when just south of the equator, 3,000 miles from the finish. The other interest was whether the French would catch the *The Great Escape*, still more than 1,000 miles ahead, still maintaining an average of around 150 miles per day; but in 36 days at sea *Kriter* had pulled back all but about 4 days of the initial 27-day advantage held by the Dutch.

The initial concern aroused by the failure of the Italian yacht *CS e RB II* to report by radio or be sighted now increased. Three weeks without news was worrying at the time *Great Britain* finished, reporting that some of the roughest waters of the voyage had been encountered in the southern Atlantic. But with the arrival of *Anaconda* the silence had now lasted more than a month since the telephone message from Geoff Cross to his home and to the *Financial Times* in Britain. He had advised that the radio was still unserviceable and that the range of the distress set was limited to 50 miles in the best conditions. Both British and Australian crews had reported seeing very few ships along their routes until they approached the European waters though the *Great Britain* crew had seen another yacht off Rio de Janeiro, probably a competitor in the Cape Town to Rio ocean race. Other yachts are a rare sight in these latitudes and one must wonder what the crew of the yacht racing to Rio must have thought, seeing an apparent competitor making tracks northwards, away from the finishing line, at best possible speed.

Adding to the concern of the race officials was the report, received via the organizers of the Whitbread triangle, that the Italian yacht *Guia III*, formerly the Australian Admiral's Cup team yacht *Gingko*, had been sunk by a killer whale when 650 miles southwest of the Cape Verde Islands. This was almost exactly halfway between the islands and the mainland of South America and not the place where help might have been readily at hand. In spite of this, and without the aid of an emergency radio, the six-man crew were in their liferaft, stocked with stores for 30 days, for only 18 hours before sighting a cargo ship, firing flares and being picked up. In one way this alleviated the fear for the Italians but in another direction it added to them. If a crew wanted to be sighted, if only to assure their friends and relatives at home, it seemed that the chances were good, or at least reasonable, and the fact that *CS e RB II* had, one hoped, passed most of the main shipping routes off South America without contact added to worries. The speed of the yacht was calculated against that of *The Great Escape*; she was estimated to cross the compulsory stop-line between Las Palmas in the Canary Islands and Barbados at about this time. The race rules insisted that if radio contact was not possible report be made ashore at either end of the line to avoid alerting international rescue assistance. The Italians reported at neither point.

Lloyds of London, in regular contact with merchant shipping throughout the world, were, as in the first leg of the race, asked to request masters of ships in the Atlantic to report sightings of the Italian yacht. Ashore there was some controversy as to the wisdom of compulsory radio reporting, but the rules of the race were emphatic. Had there been no such rule then there would have been less concern. Yachtsmen often put to sea on long voyages with a low-powered radio and merely details of the approximate time of arrival at their destination. Until this time is passed, and often well passed, no real worry is aroused. If reporting is compulsory, then concern obviously mounts when the estimated time at a stop-line is exceeded and no report is received. Responsibility begins to fall on the shoulders of the organizers in equal proportions to the anxiety felt by friends and relatives.

On 10 March, 54 days out from Sydney, *Kriter* had met light weather; she had already slowed appreciably during the previous week but the cost was shown on this particular day. The position of *Kriter*, just over 1,000 miles south of the Azores, was identical to that of *Great Britain* on day 54 from Sydney. The chase for the record was now well and truly in the balance, the forecast for the final 2,000 miles gave promise of westerlies and *Kriter*, lighter after many of her stores had been consumed, was known to be capable of the 9-knot average needed to bring her to Dover inside the new record time set by the British. Two days later they had moved little, and struggled to the northwest, rather than north or even northeast, but the weather in the Azores area, still producing the easterlies that had slowed *Anaconda* in the Channel, was giving fresh westerlies further south, and with eight days remaining *Kriter* was a day behind the British time. However, the expected southwesterlies filled: 58 days from Sydney and $6\frac{1}{2}$ days from the record they were back level with *Great Britain* on time, while the French observers, with the honour of France apparently at stake, were predicting a difference one way or the other of hours and minutes at Dover.

While the French were chasing the record of the British, as well as that

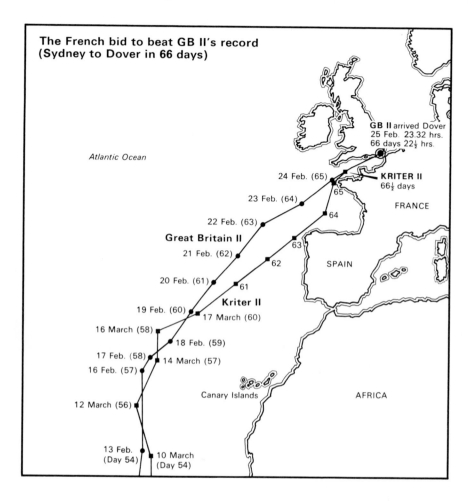

The French bid to beat GB II's record (Sydney to Dover in 66 days)

Atlantic Ocean

GB II arrived Dover 25 Feb. 23.32 hrs. 66 days 22½ hrs.

24 Feb. (65)

KRITER II 66½ days

65

23 Feb. (64)

FRANCE

64

22 Feb. (63)

Great Britain II

63

21 Feb. (62)

62

SPAIN

20 Feb. (61)

61

Kriter II

19 Feb. (60)

17 March (60)

16 March (58)

18 Feb. (59)

17 Feb. (58)

14 March (57)

16 Feb. (57)

Canary Islands

AFRICA

12 March (56)

13 Feb. (Day 54)

10 March (Day 54)

of the *Patriarch*, the Dutch were now known to be to the west of the track of *Kriter* and approximately the same distance from Dover. *Kriter* had therefore, recovered the lost 27 days from them and it became apparent that the two yachts would finish within hours of each other. Olivier de Kersauson and his navigator Yves Oliveaux chose a course well to the east of that taken either by *Great Britain* or *Anaconda* as they passed Cape Finisterre and entered Biscay, a course dictated by the prevailing wind and the need for maximum speed, but a course that would cost them their new record if the wind shifted from the west to northwest as forecast by the experts at the British meteorological centre at Bracknell. While *Great Britain* had passed Finisterre almost 300 miles to the west, the French were in sight of the high mountains that rise behind the Spanish coastline. She was maintaining the required speed, but at dawn on 22 March, 34 hours from the new record, she was still 100 miles southwest of the Isle of Ushant and being headed slightly by the wind as it veered to the north.

There was still a chance but next day, with *Kriter* round Ushant and into the Channel and still helped by fresh winds from the western sector, the shipping forecast predicted easterly gales; these materialized and then a calm, lying between the two weather patterns, stopped the French in their tracks west of Alderney. Julian Gildersleeve, the English crew member who had handled most of the radio work, told the waiting world that they had covered 10 miles in the wrong direction, but further north and west the Dutch aboard *The Great Escape* were still riding the following westerlies, much to the chagrin of the French. The more easterly course close to the coast of northwest Spain and then directly to Ushant probably cost the French crew their last chance of winning the new record either for the second leg, or for the full distance around the world which required them to beat the British time to Dover by the $6\frac{1}{2}$ hours that *Great Britain* had led them into Sydney. Had they been further west when the winds veered from west towards the north, de Kersauson and his crew could have taken a more easterly course when headed, but their course to round the Brittany peninsula had to be north, or even something to the west of this, so they were trapped by the headwinds, while away out to the northwest the Dutch were able to maintain a reach, the wind swinging from astern to abeam, and lost little speed or time.

When the crucial time of 4.04 p.m. G.M.T. passed on Tuesday 24 March, *Kriter* was still 150 miles from Dover fighting six hours of westerly running tide between Dartmouth and the Channel Islands. Already a large crowd of French supporters and journalists had gathered at Dover as well as many of the crew who had sailed *Great Britain*. Dennis Cooke, a young Leading Rating with the Royal Navy Fleet Air Arm in Scotland, seemed to have spent much of his free time since the return of *Great Britain* travelling one way or the other by rail between Dover and Scotland, but as a first-leg crewman who had spent longer than anyone else in Australia, he had many friends on all the yachts.

Once through the frustrations and calms of the western Channel, *Kriter*, with *The Great Escape* to the north, picked up westerly winds once more and covered the final 150 miles in a little over 16 hours to reach Dover at 10.20 a.m. on 25 March. She had beaten the old Clipper time by almost 2 days, and had failed to beat the British record for the return voyage from Sydney by only 35½ hours, and for the total circumnavigation by 42 hours. While Dover rocked to the spontaneous hospitality of the yacht club and the enthusiastic citizens of a town used to transient Frenchmen (though not those who had arrived directly from the other side of the world), the gallant Dutch were approaching the finish in their turn. Helped by the freshening westerlies, they were rolling up the Channel at the best possible speed for their yacht while the staff of the Royal Cinque Ports Yacht Club prepared for a second celebration and the sponsors of *Kriter* arranged a further evening celebration at the hotel across the road. That same evening the Dover lifeboat put to sea once more to meet the Dutch and escorted them into Dover through the western harbour entrance to the accompaniment of thundering maroons and the growl of the fog horns at the pierhead. While the Dutch achievement had been overshadowed by the focus of attention on the French attempt to re-establish a new record, it was a fine achievement none the less and they had covered the distance from Sydney in 95 days, 5 days better than the average run accredited to the Clipper ships, and had completed a voyage that, a few years earlier, would have caused a sensation in sailing circles.

The celebrations at Dover, where Olivier de Kersauson made a memorable speech in which he said he was now convinced that God was British, were enhanced further by the news that *CS e RB II* had been sighted.

The request to Lloyds of London had produced no news, even though the urgency of the request had been strengthened and after a lapse of 40 days Naval Attachés in London were approached by the race officials. Before the race started there had been a meeting in London between the race officers and the Naval Attachés at the London embassies of countries whose waters might be passed during the race, or whose ships might be in waters through which the yachts might sail; interest in helping, if needed, was spontaneous and unreserved, and when the call for help did eventually reach them, the sincerity of the offer was to become a reality. Within two days of alerting ships in both the northern and southern Atlantic waters, the Russian embassy reported to the race office that one of their ships, the *Alexei Shukov*, had sighted *CS e RB II* 800 miles south of the Azores making good progress to the north and that all was well aboard, although the yacht's main radio, as suspected, was still inoperable. Other embassies, notably the Argentinian and Brazilian, had already been assisting with the search by keeping special radio listening watches from their shore bases in South America.

72. H.R.H. Princess Alexandra, who met the crews before
the start, presents prizes to Roy Mullender, left, and Mike
Gill, right, for the second and first leg victories at the official
prize-giving at Trinity House, London

The French and Dutch crews spent a time adjusting to shore life and then sailed from Dover, *Kriter* to London and the Dutch to Holland, something of a sadness for the Dutch yachtsmen who had hoped to spend a few days at the St Katherine's Haven, the centre for the post-race receptions and festivities in London. Having sailed around the world and survived the voyage back from southern New Zealand to Sydney without their rudder, the French were almost to meet their Waterloo in the Thames estuary where *Kriter* ran onto a sandbank as the tide fell. Several hours later her crew were nonchalantly strolling around their yacht as she lay on her side on the dry sand, and others aboard prepared a meal with the galley canted over at 40 degrees, but they reached St Katherine's none the worse for the experience and decamped from the yacht to the opulence of the Tower Hotel in preparation for the official prize giving reception where H.R.H. Princess Alexandra, who had met the crews prior to their voyage, was able to meet them once more. It was an evening full of warmth and informality that was so much a part of the Clipper Race wherever the crews met.

Unfortunately the date of the official prize-giving was decided before the yachts reached Australia and the prizes were distributed before the Italian yacht had reached Dover. There had been hopes that they would have finished before the 2 April as, indeed, they would have if they had averaged the same speed as the Dutch from the position south of the Azores where the Russians had sighted them. Sadly, they were trapped in an area of calms near the Azores and scarcely moved for an entire week. They crossed the line late in the evening of 5 April and the Dover welcome awaited them, though it must be admitted that some of the fervour had disappeared from the festivities. The *CS e RB II* had covered the 13,500 miles in 105 days, including their enforced stop in the Falklands, but the time for the voyage seemed relatively immaterial to this crew. More important was that they sailed around the world sharing among themselves their experiences in four of the seven seas of the world. The Italians, like the Dutch, made a remarkable achievement. If it lost any significance it was only because sailing around the world is, amazingly, beginning to be taken for granted.

11 The Race in Retrospect

After Leg 2 the skippers had a debriefing, as they had after Leg 1, in which problems, experiences and advice were exchanged. Extracts from the debriefing follow.

Sails

Mike Gill: I don't know how we stood in the time of preparation we had before the race, with other competitors; I think we probably had more time than most people, certainly than Olivier, but I think that the time we did spend preparing was very well spent. We had problems due to the lack of money, but the time getting to know the boat and to train the crews prior to the race was invaluable and I think showed throughout the whole of *G.B. II*'s circumnavigation. We also had time to sort out a lot of problems in, and choosing of, items of equipment that we might have bought on speck, as it were, and to sort out the sort of sails that we wanted which was another thing that one cannot get off the peg for a boat of that size. We have to go out and to find out how the boat goes and then order the sails we want to suit the conditions we think we are going to meet. I think our appreciation of the conditions that we were going to meet was over-estimated, we expected more than we were given by Mother Nature, and so we allowed, or rather over-estimated, for strong weather. I think this is a sensible and safe thing to do, but I think we probably missed out slightly on not having enough light-weather sails. Of the middle range of sails, the normal running spinnaker and normal genoas, we went towards the heavier rather than the lighter when we had money to buy one or the other.

John Roome: * You could have approached it more like yachtsmen and less like Antarctic voyagers.

Mike Gill: I think we were approaching it as survivors, from my point of view, on the first leg because I wasn't experienced enough to make a decision or even have the money to make a decision that would cater for every situation.

Roy Mullender: Mike asked me a question a few nights ago and I've had time to think of the answer, and that is that Mike, you were saying that you wished you had more light-weather sails and that you thought we'd overdone it but, in fact, how many serviceable spinnakers, for example, did you arrive with in Sydney?

* Race Committee Chairman.

149

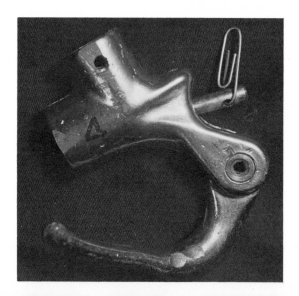

73, 74.　Several metal fittings used to attach spinnakers to halyards broke, causing severe damage and sometimes total loss of the sail. The failures were due to weak materials and faulty casting. The crew avoided using the fittings by tying sails straight onto halyards with a bowline knot

Mike Gill: We asked for a spinnaker to be made for us especially for very heavy weather, and the maker somewhat rashly guaranteed it up to 35 knots and it blew out under very easy conditions; whereas our light-weather sails blew out under conditions, or rather gave way, under relatively more easy conditions. I think we did have enough heavy-weather sails; we had two mains on board, one of which had been round the world already, and was still fit to drive us about a quarter of the way very efficiently and still set rather better than the new one. I think we were well equipped for heavy-weather sails. I think personally I had wanted to err in favour of heavy-weather sails; I hadn't put enough trail into the lighter-weight sails. Certainly when we were engulfed in the Doldrums, for a very short time I must admit, we had only one spinnaker that would set at all, one genoa that would do anything at all – as soon as that was damaged so were our chances, and I think this is the critical period, getting through the Doldrums, probably more than any other period in the race. We were fortunate, and all the other boats in the race were fortunate. It could have been a very different sort of year and a much more critical period than it was for us. In general, I think we erred in favour of rather heavy sails, and so we were lucky.

Anthony Churchill: * Do you need a different kind of sail for this kind of race, I mean a light-weather sail with a much heavier tabling?

Roy Mullender: Talking to Mike on the radio, he recommended in fact that we should make the regular spinnaker, which is a Banks Radial, heavier than the one he had on board. I went to see Bruce personally as an old friend and I said, come on Bruce, I want something better than this. We chatted, and we took it up to $2\frac{1}{2}$-ounce American regular spinnaker, and I said 'Look, please could you do the quality as you would for your own.' We had a treble stitch spinnaker with a lot of trouble taken over the tabling and the reinforcement points, and that was an extremely good spinnaker. In fact, we carried that spinnaker in almost any weather conditions, and we didn't use the light spinnaker at all. On the whole of our leg we used that spinnaker on almost every occasion we were able to and it was only destroyed for us in the end, and then only marginally, when the stainless steel V-shackle on the head snapped, and that was a half-inch V-bracket, and it fell down and got damaged coming down; so that spinnaker would be my choice again.

Olivier de Kersauson: In my opinion, there is not a spinnaker worthy of the name to go and sail south because I ask my sail-maker, 'Spinnaker – will he be able to take 50 knots of wind?' and then they all break at 35. There will be quite a new conception for this kind of sail because we only succeed to drive the boat at 14 knots average downwind for two or three hours and after, everything was break-ing. The use of conception of spinnakers like these for what we use in a race like

* Race Committee member.

Fastnet. We don't have anything for sailing south and you're always in between wearing a spinnaker which will be too much or wearing a jib and fore which will be too slow.

Roy Mullender: I remember well one period of time when our major problem was keeping the spinnakers up in the air, one corner would let go, or the other, all for different reasons – we never had the same pattern twice. We had about six occasions when the spinnaker detached itself from the mast on its own, and every time in difficult circumstances. You got to the point when you started to worry about something breaking. I remember one occasion when we had 18, gusting up into 25 knots, over the decks running fast when I distinctly said to myself that if the wind got up another 10 knots we were not going to get the spinnaker down, so let's for exercise, take it down now. We had a fine exercise I must say, in the middle of the night, but we got it down without damaging it. But it was extremely difficult.

Mike Gill: This is where the training came in, and time on training, and you had a crew which was used to taking a spinnaker down in heavy weather. You would take it that one, two or three knots further, and be fairly confident that you would get it down in reasonable order. I know I personally drove through our very best spinnaker in the South Indian Ocean and felt very ashamed at doing so, but I didn't think it was the wind strength that would actually blow it out. We were going so well at the time.

Julian Gildersleeve: * The sails are the thing that push you the whole way around the world. If you did not have sails, you would not move. Your weather conditions change the whole time, wherever you are, however you are. It becomes a daily way of life, but your sails, and how much sail you can possibly hang out, control how fast you go, and you try and work in the ultimate limit between breaking sails and not breaking sails, and pushing the boat and not pushing the boat. Just try and work in the limit – if your sails can stand it, if the boat and mast can support your sails, you will go that bit faster.

Safety

Mike Gill: From the publicity angle of this race, none of us have come back with any particularly hairy stories and having feared for the safety of our ships, although Olivier lost a rudder his hull was intact so there was not any danger of sinking. Nobody, as far as I can gather, has ever feared for the safety of the ship. Has anyone rolled over?

John Roome: Anaconda rolled over.

Mike Gill: Do you think that if the hull was not damaged there was no danger of sinking?

* *Kriter II*'s English crewman and radio operator.

152

Lou Davidson:* The only damage was really that the main went aross one of the seams. The fibreglass casing of the liferaft was stoved in. Possibly that could be a point if you are going down to these terrible waters and heavier seas. Possibly a stronger liferaft cocoon would be a worthy consideration.

Olivier de Kersauson: The liferaft is useless.

John Roome: You say the liferaft was useless, but it has just saved the crew of *Guia*.

Olivier de Kersauson: Yes, but that was in tropical weather, which is quite different.

John Roome: Yes, but you have to go through all parts of the world – you could sink anywhere.

Olivier de Kersauson: A liferaft between south of New Zealand and Cape Horn is something useless; after that, it starts to be useful, eventually. In this part of the world I remember we had been sailing *Kriter* in deep permanent fog, no visibility and the only things we were getting were the crack of icebergs – so they give you the feeling that a liferaft in that – no way. We went into bad visibility in areas with the icebergs some five miles long, and the only picture we could see was fog, and double fog for seven days non stop. We had not seen a star for seven days, neither the sun. I mean what would you be doing in a liferaft in that. No way, forget it. In the fog we were sometimes carrying her, pushing and praying. Sometimes I prayed more than I pushed.

Anthony Churchill: So when you hear the crash of an iceberg, what do you do? Do you take down your spinnaker?

Olivier de Kersauson: No, you don't do anything, you just go on. If you hear the crack that means it's cracking behind you. For days it has been really, well I won't say scary because I am very courageous as everyone knows, but it has kept my mind very busy, because it was the worst condition of sailing that I have ever had in my whole life, which is very long, I mean at sea. Really it was awful. There was no way to escape from that, when we were going north the fog was following us, going south, I think. I think the more south we got the higher were the icebergs we met so it was always playing in between the 55 and 57 [degrees] and no way to excape from that.

Radio

John Roome: Anaconda had quite a lot of electrical equipment you perhaps wished you didn't have to cart about.

Lou Davidson: Possibly, electronic equipment these days is so advanced of course that the weight is not a great factor. We didn't use it at all. But I think it could have been better protected certainly. It was damaged by sea water and sea

* *Anaconda II*'s navigator.

air. I think that was mainly because it just wasn't built for a yacht or wasn't designed for yacht use.

Mike Gill: Could *Kriter* have, as a case in point here? I don't know the details but they had a marine radio which in fact wasn't very marinized. Julian probably knows more about it – a bit of spray and . . .

Julian Gildersleeve: The main radio. It's a marinized radio but any electronic equipment on a boat to start with is a problem, bearing in mind electricity and water don't mix – you get a dead short between the two and that's it – finished. Trying to separate the two is something else.

Mike Gill: We carried as a normal, as our everyday communications radio with our base in England, a radio which could be dropped in water and immersed for several hours and still come out fighting.

Julian Gildersleeve: There's no way our radio could do that. Our radio, if it got in contact with water would start blowing fuses or puffs of smoke at you, burning transistors. It worked, it's a very, very good radio but you get problems, it gives you headaches the whole day long.

Mike Gill: People call these marinized radios and they are intended for use on yachts but in fact they are not waterproof or even condensation-proof.

Julian Gildersleeve: Our radio was a marinized radio, supposedly. It was in a very protected place from water. There was virtually no way water could get at it, apart from condensation. But condensation dripped in and the whole thing went rusty. You need a very different radio from one you would use for a lifetime in the Channel compared to one that will be virtually wet for two months, and there's no way you can avoid it.

Reporting Positions

Olivier de Kersauson: I have some problems to speak your language, but let me talk to just say I think we had a lot of problems for some time and we are trying very hard to report every day. Julian has been working hard every day to try and talk. There was never any tactical thing from *Kriter* to hide its position. Sometimes our position must have been higher, I wish to deny that because it was not a very good run. But we played that race fair enough, not to never hide. That's all I want to say. I think that the analysis that was made was not very fair to us and I can't accept it. I never lie – except when it is very necessary.

John Roome: While we are on radio, could we just go to this thing which before the race was the most controversial rule that we had which was the stop-line. The rule about the stop-line that you have to stop if you haven't reported was opposed by a number of competitors.

Dirk Nauta: When I heard everything about *CS e RB II* we were very close to each other and he had trouble with his radio I think because his radio was, just got wet, troubled by water and spray so he could not make contact and he has for four days been in the Falkland islands and couldn't get it repaired and what do you have to do, call other ports. If I had been on *CS e RB* what would I have done is go straight through to Dover.

John Roome: But you appreciate that the point of the rule was that if someone leaves Australia and we don't hear another thing, we can't do anything to alert help for maybe 120 days and he might be just out of sight of Sydney. This is the object of the exercise.

Dirk Nauta: I think the primary responsibility is always the skipper's, not the Race Committee's. The skipper is driving the boat.

John Roome: There was a time when *CS e RB*, when she sailed from the Falklands having apparently repaired her radio which was the story that came back, forty-five days later, no one had heard a word from her. There had been no sight of her. *Guia* went down in minutes and her crew were found by, O.K., good luck, within eighteen hours and she was 700 miles from the nearest land.
CS e RB hadn't even been sighted. People had sighted some of you on the way round the world, both legs, and had reported sightings even though they hadn't been asked to do so but nothing had been heard for forty-five days, which as Mary Pera, Secretary of the R.O.R.C., said could put her anywhere between Wolf Rock and Falkland. Where do we start looking? And then we alerted the Embassies and luckily the Russians came up with a sighting within forty-eight hours. But still there was no report from *CS e RB* of any sort or any sighting or any request to Lloyds to report their position.

Mike Gill: I think you must get skippers to sign a disclaimer if you're worried about this to say, don't look for me.

Olivier de Kersauson: There are two points. Each will be examined very carefully. Imagine a skipper fighting like hell, driving his boat day and night non-stop, having a radio problem. We say, get lost radio, we don't want to hear about that God damned thing. And he's pushing hard, radio has no wind, radio has no sails, radio has no seamanship. I will never forget that. I will never forget that on a point for a man who is driving hard and making everything to go faster, the fact that the God-damned machine does not work, he can't even take care – blow it, put fire on it, do anything. Does everybody understand? The two points of view must be realized; they are very different points and must not be mixed. Don't forget that. Those men are sailing and are manoeuvring and skippering more than broadcasting – finish. Everybody knows that everybody is doing his best to give news for everybody because it is the interest of the race. As a skipper I was not for that before the race but now I am for it because I think it can be very nice to know that the weather there – it gives you the feeling that you are competing in different boats, it increased the great sailing pleasure you have but don't put the radio over that, the radio must always be, if we want to keep the sailing in mind, behind at some stage which its usefulness is very nice for the family but nothing to do with the race.

Anthony Churchill: If there had not been stop-lines *CS e RB* need not have put into the Falkland Islands, we would not have heard, as of this day, bar again this Russian ship, what had happened to her since she left Sydney. He did not have to stay there and repair it. He could have gone straight on to the next stop-line.

John Roome: Could I just say this, as Chairman of the Race Committee, if you like? It's all very well you saying 'all right sign disclaimers', I mean if you want to sail around the world just by yourselves, by all means do it. You can do it without any radio on board at all, but if you enter into a race that people are running, then we are responsible, to some extent, for what goes on. We are bound to be. We have got to keep an eye on the thing and you are not just doing your own little cruise – you are entering into a race with other people and with organizers.

There had been times during the initial conception of the *Financial Times* Clipper Race, during the months that seemed to grow shorter as the start approached, and even during the race itself, when it seemed the event might become overshadowed by problems – often problems outside the control of organizers or crews – or by shortage of time; but by sheer effort, some luck, and the help of many who simply wanted to contribute something to the event, the race became the experience of a lifetime for the crews and enthralled thousands of people around the world. Who could have predicted that two yachts, from a small field of four, would reach Australia merely hours apart? Who, except for those who had met Olivier de Kersauson and his team, could have predicted the chase that was to take place after that sad storm-ridden parting of the ways when *Great Britain II* left *Kriter II* to struggle back to Sydney? While the race itself produced moments of excitement, fear, hilarity and frustration for the crews, it touched many more than the hundred or so people who either sailed in it, or supplied the mountain of support and back-up for the yachts.

The week-long Festival of Sail that preceded it enabled thousands of youngsters to meet, with the bond of sailing as their common denominator. It enabled thousands of others to witness an unforgettable sight of square-rigged ships, yachts and barges of every size and shape moored in the heart of the world's oldest seafaring city.

In Australia, where the specially formed Clipper Race Australian Committee prepared for the arrival and departure of the yachts, the friendships made and the memories of unexpected and unplanned hospitality, many that no one could have predicted, will last those who were there a lifetime. The race gave an opportunity for many who might never have had a chance even to meet the sea and seafarers to become involved with men and women who had rounded the Horn.

Among the crews, characters were noticeably changed. The quiet younger person found a boost of self-confidence, together with the quiet reassurance of knowing that no description of the voyage was really necessary in order to prove anything. Stolid men with a reputation for calm in a harassing moment came home with an even deeper understanding of life and their fellows. It would be inaccurate to avoid mention of other factors that emerged or to pretend that in every yacht life ran smooth as clockwork. This was not the case, and there can be no one naïve enough to imagine otherwise. One or two who had planned the full voyage left their yachts in Sydney. Either they realized that they were not as happy in their yachts as they had hoped, or felt it better for the rest of the crew that they stayed behind. These were as brave individual decisions as the one made to continue; they were treated by the crews as such and there was never any loss of face or acrimony. All yachts had their moments of friction, sometimes between individuals, occasionally between watches; they are bound to occur when groups of sixteen, thirteen or even seven people are cramped together in conditions that at times allowed only survival.

What of the crews themselves? The people who sailed in the Clipper Race were as varied a cross-section as any. *Great Britain II* was manned entirely by personnel from the British armed forces, selected after intensive evaluation not only of sailing experience but of the ability to be compatible with their fellow crew, and as far as position aboard the yacht was concerned, without regard to rank. Mike Gill who skippered the team on the first leg is a captain in the Royal Engineers and former navigator of the yacht *British Soldier* in the Sydney to Rio de Janeiro leg of the Whitbread race; he had the quiet Scot David Leslie, a Staff Sergeant in the Royal Electrical and Mechanical Engineers, as his Chief Mate and John Bagnall, who retired as a Brigadier in the Royal Artillery, as his navigator. The divergence of military skills will be seen from the crews lists (Appendix 3, pages 187–201), but sailing skills diverged as much. Chief Petty Officer John Parfoot, a Medical Technician in the Royal

Navy, was not only one of the heavyweight winch winders, but doctor as well as dentist, and was called upon to fill a damaged tooth for Colin Wagstaff, an infantry captain sailing as a mate and purser.

On the second leg, the *Great Britain II* crew list was led by the photogenic Chief Petty Officer Roy Mullender, a veteran of Naval Sail Training and head of Naval Sail Training administration when he was appointed to the task. This senior non-commissioned officer led a team of yachtsmen who included an infantry major, two brace of army captains, a squadron leader and a full hand of senior non-commissioned officers. Only David Leslie and Royal Marine radio operator Keith Powell sailed both legs.

Olivier de Kersauson was faced with an entirely different problem when selecting his crew for *Kriter II*, the time factor here again playing a crucial part. There was a wealth of experienced men available in France, but the decision to take part was late and not all those he wanted could take eight months away from work at short notice. While *Great Britain II* soon achieved a chain of command and delegation of tasks, life aboard *Kriter* was a sharply-pointed pyramid, with de Kersauson at the top, supported by bosun Georges Commarmond. Initially it appeared that all the weight of decision fell on the skipper's shoulders, though the crew more than compensated for this by turning to the hundreds of tasks facing them with skills and enthusiasm that often outweighed the prob-lems themselves. There was never any doubt in anyone's mind as to who was in charge though there seemed some doubts on occasions as to where other responsibilities lay.

Doi Malingri aboard *CS e RB II* had the least trouble in gathering his crew. He only wanted seven people including himself and his friend Elnora Waring, and chose Paolo Mascheroni who sailed the final leg of the Whitbread race aboard the first *CS e RB* with him. Other than that he acquired crew as he sailed the transatlantic race and the preceding voyage to America, and he and his team were perhaps the most compat-ible if also the most cavalier of the race.

The crew of the Dutch ketch, *The Great Escape*, were chosen from applicants enlisted through the sailing school which owned the yacht, most of them paying a full charter fee for taking part. Again they were a broad cross-section of life and a sure sign of the lessons learned must be that when the little yacht, the smallest in the race, arrived at Dover after both legs had been completed, the accommodation below decks was in first-class order.

One of the Dutch yachtsmen summed up the underlying feelings of those who took part when he said of the race as a whole, 'It is not what I gained by taking part, but what I have not missed that really counts.'

Appendices

1 Race Rules

(including Notice of Race)

1   *Rules and regulations*

The race will be sailed under I.Y.R.U. Racing Rules, these General Conditions, Clipper Race Special Regulations, the I.O.R. Mk III and the Sailing Instructions.

2   *Starting times*

The race will take place in two legs:

(a) London–Sydney via Cape of Good Hope, starting on the morning of Sunday 31 August 1975.
(b) Sydney–London via Cape Horn, starting at noon on Sunday 21 December 1975.

3   *Eligibility*

The race is open to yachts with I.O.R. Mk III ratings between 40 and 70 feet inclusive, complying with Clipper Race Special Regulations.

4   *I.Y.R.U. Rule 26*

Names of yachts will not normally be regarded as contravening I.Y.R.U. Rule 26 provided they are proper names and not advertising slogans. In any case of doubt, proposed names should be submitted to the Race Committee as early as possible before the race. When submitting a name any commercial connection with it known to the owner or skipper of the yacht must be made clear. The Race Committee reserves the right to decline any entry under I.Y.R.U. Rule 1.4.

5   *Minimum crew*

Every yacht shall race with a crew of at least six persons.

6   *Navigation methods*

Any method of navigation is allowed, so long as it uses information available to all: individual pre-arranged help such as weather forecasts from nearby shipping or aircraft, is prohibited.

7   *Electronic aids*

There is no restriction on the type and usage of electronic aids carried on board, provided they do not contravene any of the Rules and Regulations.

8   *Entries*

Written on the official entry form entries shall be sent to:

The *Financial Times* Clipper Race Office,
34 Buckingham Palace Road,
London, S W 1 W 0 R E, England.

Closing dates	*Entries close*	*Race starts*
(i) First leg, London–Sydney	31 May 1975	31 August 1975
(ii) Second leg, Sydney–London	21 September 1975	21 December 1975

Entry fees: £100 one leg only, or £150 both legs. Entry fees (payable to the Royal Ocean Racing Club), must be received before the appropriate closing date.

Late entries, on payment of double entry fees, may be accepted at the discretion of the Race Committee.

Rating certificates shall be lodged with the Race Committee before the appropriate closing date, unless there are exceptional circumstances in which case the Race Committee may agree to accept the certificate at a date not later than 48 hours before the start.

9   *Prizes and awards*   *Given by*

Will include the following:

Financial Times 'Patriarch' *Trophy* to the yacht which makes the fastest two-way passage. The trophy is a model of the clipper ship *Patriarch*	*Financial Times*
Fastest passage London–Sydney	*Financial Times*
Best handicap passage London–Sydney	Royal Ocean Racing Club
Fastest passage Sydney–London	*Financial Times*
Best handicap passage Sydney–London	Royal Ocean Racing Club
Sir Francis Chichester Logbook: Leather bound reproduction of the log kept by Sir Francis Chichester as he rounded the Horn in his epic single-handed voyage around the world. For the best kept log in the race	Lady Chichester

The *'Cutty Sark' Prize*: A silver salver for the yacht coming second overall on elapsed time for the whole race	The *Cutty Sark* Society
The *Little Ship Club Prize* for the most outstanding act of seamanship notified to the committee of the club in London	The Little Ship Club
Clipper Race Sailors' Medals awarded to each person for completing each leg of the course	*Financial Times*

10   *Handicap system*

Time-on-distance using the following formula:

Basic Speed Figure (B.S.F.) in seconds per mile =
$$\frac{5143}{\sqrt{\text{Rating}} + 3.5}$$

11   *Sailing instructions will be issued at:*

(a) Race Headquarters, St Katherine's Haven, London, during the week prior to 31 August 1975 and

(b) Race Headquarters, Ruchcutters Bay, Sydney, during the week prior to 21 December 1975.

12   *Check-in periods*

Each yacht is required to report to:

(a) Race Headquarters, St Katherine's Haven, London at or before 1200 on Saturday 23 August 1975 and

(b) Race Headquarters, Rushcutters Bay, Sydney, at, or before 1200 on Monday 15 December 1975,
for pre-race inspections; between this time and the start of the race at least three members of the racing crew must be present and the yacht will be at the disposal of the Race Committee.

13   *Radio reporting*

(i) Each yacht is required to send regular position reports to Race Control in London or Sydney, via commercial radio stations or other means, as follows (commercial charges (not ship station) for handling official position reports will be met by the *Financial Times*):

Table 1. Frequency of reports

London–Sydney		Required reports
(a)	London River to Lat. 45° North	Daily
(b)	Lat. 45° North to Long. 100° East	Twice weekly
(c)	Long. 100° East to Long. 140° East	Daily
(d)	Long. 140° East to Sydney Harbour	Twice daily

Sydney–London		Required reports
(e)	Sydney Harbour to 170° West	Daily
(f)	170° West to 80° West	Twice weekly
(g)	80° West to 60° West or 50° South	Daily
(h)	60° West or 50° South to 45° North	Twice weekly
(i)	45° North to 48° North	Daily
(j)	48° North to London River	Twice daily

Any failure to report according to this schedule must be reported in writing to the Race Committee immediately after the race, and action may be taken under General Condition 17.

(ii) *Preliminary lines and stop-lines* These lines are established as follows:

(a) *Preliminary lines* (unless otherwise stated) are parallel with stop-lines and 500 miles nearer to the start of the appropriate leg.
(b) *Stop-lines* Where only one point of origin is given for a stop-line, its remote end shall be taken as the point at which the line meets a coastline or permanent ice pack.

Table 2. Stop Lines

Point(s) of origin		True bearing of line (if from single point of origin)	Reporting port
(i)	Freetown, Sierra Leone	315°	Freetown
(ii)	Rio de Janeiro, Brazil, through St Helena, eastwards through Ascension Island		Rio de Janeiro or St Helena
(iii)	Cape Town, South Africa	180°	Cape Town
(iv)	Perth, Western Australia	225°	Perth
(v)	Wellington, New Zealand or Auckland, New Zealand	180° 360°	Wellington Auckland

Table 2. (continued)

Point(s) of origin	True bearing of line (if from single point of origin)	Reporting port
(vi) Port Stanley, Falkland Islands (Preliminary line in this case shall be longitude 70° West)	180° or 270°	Port Stanley
(vii) Las Palmas, Canary Islands to Trinidad, Barbados		Las Palmas or Trinidad

(c) Regardless of her obligations under Table 1 above, every yacht is required to communicate at least one position report to Race Control London or Race Control Sydney, whenever the yacht finds herself between a *preliminary* line and a *stop*-line as shown in Table 2. A yacht which passes a *stop*-line without so doing will be disqualified. If a yacht cannot communicate by any means she will be expected to proceed to the reporting port listed above, and there to:

(a) inform Race Control London or Race Control Sydney of her whereabouts, and

(b) put her communications equipment into working order before proceeding.

(iii) *Search and rescue* The arrangements described here will help Race Control to decide whether, and if so, when and where to request Search and Rescue assistance.

14 *Flags*

Each yacht shall show International Code Flag 'P' of not less size than 15″ × 12″ (about 40 cm × 30 cm) prominently displayed (if possible on the permanent backstay) at all times from the start of the relevant check-in period until six hours after the start of each leg, and when approaching and crossing the finishing line. National ensigns may be worn throughout.

15 *Automatic, mechanical and wind-vane devices* for steering are prohibited.

16   *Use of engines*

(a) An engine may be used for charging batteries, pumping bilges or supplying power for weighing anchor.

(b) An engine may be used for propulsion to recover a man overboard, to render assistance, to avoid collision, or in any other grave emergency but in every case full details must be reported on the declaration.

17   *Rule infringement*

If the Race Committee considers that an infringement of the rules has been committed, it may:

(a) disqualify the yacht, or

(b) impose such other penalty as it sees fit.

18   *Ratings*

(a) A yacht must have a valid I.O.R. Mk III rating. A copy of the rating certificate must be kept on board.

(b) The ratings of all competitors will be posted with sailing instructions on the notice board of the headquarters from which the race is started. The rating so posted at the time of the start shall be final for that leg of the race except that it may be protested by another yacht entered for the same race provided that the protester lodges written notice of intention to protest together with a deposit of £50.00 at the race head-quarters before the start.

(c) Notwithstanding (b), above, the Race Committee, under I.Y.R.U. rule 14.1 shall have a discretionary power to correct errors in ratings.

19   *Sail numbers*

Sail numbers allotted by a national authority must be carried on the mainsail, the spinnaker and on every headsail of which the L.P. meas-urement is equal to or exceeds 1.3 times the measurement of J. The sail number of the size shown on the mainsail must be displayed by alternative means if none of the numbered sails is set, and must be displayed in the lifelines on the side of the yacht which faces the Race Committee at the start, and at the finish. Dimensions should be as specified by the yacht's national authority.

20   *List of entries*

As far as possible names and ratings of competitors will be included in sailing instructions supplied to yachts, but these may not be complete or exact.

21   *Crew list*

Each yacht must hand in a crew list, complete with passport-type photograph of each crew member, at least 48 hours before each start.

22   *Medical declaration*

Each skipper will be required to sign a declaration before each start to confirm that he has satisfied himself that every member of his crew including himself, are to the best of his knowledge and belief, physically and mentally fit to undertake the voyage. (Facilities for medical checks will be available at London and Sydney but skippers are advised to undertake preliminary checks well in advance.)

SPECIAL REGULATIONS

1.0   *Introduction*

These regulations are based upon Category 1 requirements of the Offshore Rating Council's publication 'Special Regulations Governing Minimum Equipment and Accommodation Standards' published 11 November 1973 and amended to 1 November 1974.

1.1   *Clipper Race only*

These regulations have been specially adapted for the *Financial Times* Clipper Race and do not necessarily apply to any other race. Where there is a difference between these regulations and those published by the O.R.C. there is a vertical line printed in the left-hand margin.

2.0   *Skipper's responsibility*

The safety of a yacht and her crew is the sole and inescapable responsibility of the skipper, who must do his best to ensure that the yacht is fully found, thoroughly seaworthy and manned by an experienced crew who are physically fit to face bad weather. He must ensure that all safety equipment is properly maintained and stowed and that the crew know where it is kept and how it is to be used.

2.1   Notice is drawn to I.Y.R.U. Rule 57, from which the following is an extract: 'No person on board a yacht when her preparatory signal was made shall leave, unless injured or ill, or for the purpose of rule 58, Rendering Assistance, except that any member of the crew may fall overboard provided that this person is back on board before the yacht continues in the race.'

An exception to this rule will be recognized only where a member of the crew leaves the yacht for urgent private or business reasons, to take no further part in that leg of the race. Such exception shall not relieve the yacht from her obligation under General Condition 5 (minimum crew 6 persons).

2.2   Neither the establishment of these special regulations, their use by sponsoring organizations, nor the inspection of a yacht under these regulations in any way limits or reduces the complete and unlimited responsibility of the skipper.

2.3   It is the sole and exclusive responsibility of each yacht to decide whether or not to start or continue to race.

3.0   *Basic standards*

3.1   Hulls of offshore racing yachts shall be self-righting, strongly built, watertight and capable of withstanding solid water and knockdowns. They must be properly rigged and ballasted, be fully seaworthy and must meet the standards set forth herein. Shrouds must never be disconnected.

'Self-righting' means that a yacht must have a positive righting arm when the masthead, with main and foresail set, touches the water.

3.2   All equipment must function properly, be readily accessible and be of a type, size and capacity suitable and adequate for the intended use and the size of the yacht, and shall meet standards accepted in the country of registry.

3.3   It will not be considered adequate for yachts simply to carry materials and tools with which to manufacture the items of equipment called for in these rules.

4.0   *Inspections*

4.1   All yachts will be inspected in London, and again in Sydney, prior to the commencement of each leg of the race. Also, the Race Committee may at its discretion, cause inspections to be carried out at any port at which the yacht may call on the race. If a yacht does not comply with these rules her entry may be rejected, or she will be liable to disqualification or penalty.

4.2   Inspectors may call for the demonstration by any member of the crew, of any of the equipment described in these rules. Attention is drawn to the final sentence in rule 2.1.

4.3   Inspectors may call for the demonstration by any member of the crew, of safety procedures in event of various emergencies.

5.0   *Special requirements for Category 1 races (see 1.0 – Introduction)*

5.1   All yachts are required to be completely self-sufficient for extended periods of time, capable of withstanding heavy storms and prepared to meet serious emergencies without the expectation of outside assistance.

6.0   *Structural features*

6.1   Hatches, companionways and ports must be essentially watertight, that is, capable of being strongly and rigidly secured. Cockpit companionways, if extended below main deck level, must be capable of being blocked off to main deck level. If cockpit opens aft to the sea, the lower edge of the companionway may not be below deck level. The blocking arrangement required by this rule must be stowed near to the companionway and must be so constructed and marked that it may be rapidly and easily fitted the correct way round, and, if more than one piece is involved, in the correct order. The blocking device must be capable of being strongly secured in place.

6.1.1   At least two exits must be available for crew members to escape from within the hull in case of fire or other emergency, and such exits shall be of adequate size to allow unimpeded passage by a crewman wearing a lifejacket.

6.2   Cockpits must be structurally strong, self-bailing and permanently incorporated as an integral part of the hull. They must be essentially watertight, that is, all openings to the hull below the main deck level must be capable of being strongly and rigidly secured.

6.2.1   The maximum cockpit volume below coamings shall not exceed 6 percent L. times B. times F.A. The cockpit sole must be at least 2 percent L. above L.W.L.

6.3   Cockpit drains adequate to drain 75 percent of each cockpit in less than five minutes, or cockpit drains in each cockpit with a combined area (after allowance for screens, if attached) of not less than the equivalent of four 2-inch (5.0 cm) drains.

6.4   Storm coverings for all windows more than two square feet in area. Such storm coverings shall be constructed from a rigid material and shall be designed and made to fit quickly, closely and securely to the outside of the windows to be protected.

6.5   Sea cocks or valves on all through-hull openings below L.W.L., except integral deck scuppers, shaft log, speed indicators, depth finders and the like, however a means of closing such openings, when necessary to do so, shall be provided. All through-hull openings shall be readily accessible from within the hull.

6.5.1   Soft wood plugs, tapered and of various sizes.

6.6   *Lifelines and pulpits*

Fixed bow pulpit (forward of headstay) and stern pulpit (unless lifelines are arranged as to adequately substitute for a stern pulpit).

Pulpits and stanchions must be through-bolted or welded, and the base thereof must not be further inboard from the edge of the working deck than 5 percent of B. max. or 6 inches (15 cm), whichever is greater. A stanchion must not be angled from the point of its attachment to the hull at more than 10 degrees from vertical throughout the length. Taut double lifelines, with upper lifelines of wire at a height of not less than 2 feet (60 cm) above the working deck, to be permanently supported at intervals of not more than 7 feet (2.15 m). A taut lanyard of synthetic rope may be used to secure lifelines, provided that when in position its length does not exceed 4 inches (10 cm). Apart from such synthetic rope lanyards, insulators may not be used as lifeline connections unless their construction is such that a metal interlock is provided which will fully maintain the strength of the lifeline in the event of physical collapse of the insulating material. Lower lifelines shall extend through the bow pulpit. Lifelines need not be affixed to the bow pulpit if they terminate at, or pass through adequately braced stanchions 2 feet (60 cm) above the working deck, set inside of and overlapping the bow pulpit, provided that the gap between the upper lifeline and the bow pulpit shall not exceed 6 inches (15 cn). Stanchion bases may not be situated outboard of the working deck.

6.6.1   *Safety harness guide lines and anchorage points*

Wire guide lines shall be fitted on deck, port and starboard of the yacht's centreline, to provide secure attachments for safety harnesses. Guide lines shall be attached to through-bolted or welded deck plates, or other suitable and strong anchorage. The lines shall if possible be fitted in such a way that a crew member, when clipped on, can move from a cockpit to the forward and to the after end of the main deck without unclipping the harness, but if the deck layout renders this impossible, additional lines shall be fitted so that a crew member can move as described with a minimum of clipping operations.

A crew member must be able to remain clipped on whilst moving laterally across the yacht on the foredeck, the afterdeck, and amidships, and if necessary additional guide lines and/or through-bolted or welded anchorage points shall be provided for this purpose.

Through-bolted or welded anchorage points, or other suitable and strong anchorage, for safety harnesses shall be provided adjacent to every hatchway, and adjacent to stations such as the helm, sheet winches and masts, where crew members work for long periods.

6.7   *Ballast and heavy equipment*

Inside ballast in a yacht shall be securely fastened in position. All other heavy internal fittings such as batteries, stoves, gas bottles, tanks, outboard motors, etc., shall be securely fastened.

6.8	Sheet winches shall be mounted in such a way that no operator is required to be substantially below deck.

7.0 *Accommodations*

7.1 Toilet, permanently installed.

7.2 Bunks, permanently installed.

7.3 Cooking stove, permanently installed with safe accessible fuel shutoff control.

7.4 Galley facilities, including sink.

7.5 Water tanks, permanently installed, dividing the water supply into at least two separate containers. At least 30 gallons of potable water for each crew member must be embarked at the start of each leg of the race. Part of the total water supply carried by each yacht shall be in at least four additional water containers which shall in aggregate contain at least 20 gallons of water, shall each be fitted with a carrying handle, strong simple closure, a floating line 8 feet (2.5 m) long, and contain sufficient air to provide flotation. These containers must be kept in a special stowage from which they can be got to the lifelines within 30 seconds.

A maximum of 10 percent of the water required by this rule may instead be carried in the form of mineral water, cola, etc. Adequate arrangements shall be made for collection of rainwater, or otherwise to provide additional extra potable water on each leg of the race.

8.0 *General equipment*

8.1 Fire extinguishers, at least three, to be installed in suitable and separate parts of the vessel. Each extinguisher shall be of a dry powder type at least 3 lb. (1.4 kg) in weight.

8.2 Fire blanket to be kept in a special holder which must be permanently installed close to the galley.

8.2.1 Bilge pumps, at least three, manually operated, one of which must be operable with all cockpit seats and all hatches and companionways closed. At least two of the bilge pumps must be securely fixed to the yacht's structure.

8.3 Anchors, two, with cables.

8.4 Self-contained, water-resistant flashlights, one for each crew member. The flashlights shall be capable of working satisfactorily both during and after total submersion in sea water, and at least two of these shall also be suitable for signalling. Adequate spare batteries and bulbs.

8.5	Medical kit, and detailed contents list. Main items of kit to be stored in individual watertight wrappings and entire kit made up and stored in watertight non-rusting container of bright distinctive colour and having positive buoyancy.
8.5.1	Medical handbooks: one copy each of: *The Ship Captain's Medical Guide* (H.M. Stationery Office) and Ward-Gardner and Roylance's *First Aid Book*, except that non-British yachts may carry in lieu, equivalent publications.
8.6	Foghorn.
8.7	Radar reflector: If the reflector is octahedral it must have a minimum diagonal measurement of 18 inches (46 cm), or if not octahedral must have an 'equivalent echoing area' of not less than 10 sq. m. The minimum effective height above water is 12 feet (4 m).
8.8	Set of International Code flags and International Code book. Each code flag shall measure at least 18 inches (46 cm) in the hoist.
8.9	Shutoff valves on all fuel tanks, including tanks which lie below the level of their associated pipes and machinery when the yacht is floating in design trim.
8.9.1	The yacht's electrical systems must be equipped with fuses or circuit breakers and be capable of being isolated.
8.9.2	At least two entirely separate methods of generating electricity (with independent prime movers), each capable of producing sufficient electrical energy to drive the yacht's main transmitter continuously on full power output independent of any batteries; each system must be suppressed so that radio transmission and reception is not unduly hampered.
8.9.3	A propulsion engine with propeller together capable of driving the yacht in calm water at a speed of at least L knots. The installation should be maintained in a condition in which it is ready for immediate use.
8.9.4	Fuel capable of propelling the yacht for at least 100 miles must be carried at the start of each leg.
8.9.5	Safe and rapid means to evacuate heavier-than-air gas from within the hull. Electrical switches and motors employed for this purpose shall be sparkproof and sealed.
9.0	*Navigation Equipment*
9.1	Compass, marine type, properly installed and adjusted.
9.2	Spare compass.

9.3   Charts, light list and piloting equipment.

9.4   Sextant, tables and accurate time piece.

9.5   Radio direction finder.

9.6   Lead line or echo sounder.

9.7   Speedometer or distance-measuring instrument.

9.8   Navigation lights, to be shown as required by the International
         Regulations for Preventing Collisions at Sea, mounted so that they
         will not be masked by sails or the heeling of the yacht. Each sidelight
         bulb must have a manufacturer's rating of at least 10 watts, or each
         sidelight must have an intensity outside the lantern of at least 1.5
         candelas. Sternlight bulbs must have a manufacturer's rating of at
         least 6 watts.

10.0   *Emergency equipment*

10.1   Emergency navigation lights with the same minimum standards as
         the lights described in 9.8.

10.2   Special storm sail(s) capable of taking the yacht to windward in heavy
         weather, including at least one heavy weather jib and reefing equip-
         ment for mainsail.

10.3   Emergency steering equipment shall include an emergency tiller, but
         in addition yachts will be required to demonstrate that a completely
         independent emergency steering arrangement can be brought into use
         and that all items of equipment necessary for its employment are
         carried on board.

10.4   Tools and spare parts, including a hacksaw, with at least ten spare
         blades, and heavy wire cutters.

10.5   Yacht's name on miscellaneous buoyant equipment, such as
         lifejackets, oars, cushions, etc. Portable sail number (dimensions not
         less than mainsail number).

10.6   Marine radio transmitter and receiver capable of communication by
         voice with shore stations up to a range of at least 4000 miles on seven
         or more frequencies in the 2, 4, 6, 8, 12, 16 and 22 MHz bands. Min-
         imum transmitter power shall be 150 watts except that the Race
         Committee may in exceptional cases permit instead a lower transmit-
         ter power, provided that

    (i) the proposed equipment is capable of transmitting by voice over the
         minimum distance required;
   (ii) permission is sought and received from the Race Committee, which
         may require the equipment to be demonstrated or delivered for

testing to its agents not less than two months prior to the start of the race.

If the regular antenna depends upon the mast, an emergency antenna must be provided.

10.7   Emergency portable self-contained radio transmitter or transmitter receiver, capable of transmitting on 2182 kHz and at least one other internationally designated distress frequency between 4 and 23 MHz, watertight and with positive buoyancy. The emergency radio must be kept in a special stowage from which it can be got to the lifelines within 30 seconds. The radio must be permanently fitted with a floating line at least 8 feet (2.5 m) in length.

10.8   One copy of *Admiralty List of Radio Signals* (A.L.R.S.) Volume 1.

11.0   *Safety equipment*

11.1   Lifejackets, one for each crew member. Each lifejacket shall *either* bear 'kite-mark' stamp of the British Standards Institution in respect of British Standard 3595, *or* shall be manufactured to similar standards and shall have a minimum total buoyancy of 35 lbf. Each lifejacket shall be fitted with a removable outer cover to protect it against wear and tear. The lifejacket shall be so designed that its use does not conflict with the wearing and use of a safety harness.

11.2   A whistle shall be attached to each lifejacket by a short lanyard, both lanyard and whistle being stowed in a special pocket easily accessible to the user with either hand.

11.2.1 An emergency watertight light shall be fitted to each lifejacket, and may consist of one of the following types (the first being preferred):
    (i) xenon flare;
   (ii) water-activated battery light;
  (iii) dry battery light.
        A personal pack of pyrotechnic flares with ejection device may be fitted to each lifejacket instead of, or in addition to the required waterproof light.

11.3   Safety harness, one for each crew member. (Minimum recommended breaking strains are given in the booklet 'Advice to Competitors' available from the *Financial Times* Clipper Race Office.) Each harness shall *either* be provided with two safety lines, *or* one safety line with an intermediate hook. Hooks on safety lines shall *either* be spring-closing snap hooks with an additional screw-up collar, *or* another suitable design with positive locking arrangement.

11.4   Liferafts with total official (not counting overload) of at least 150 percent number of crew, arranged as follows:

11.4.1	Liferaft(s) representing 100 percent crew capacity (not counting overload) must be carried in special stowage(s) opening immediately to the deck containing liferaft(s) only, and from which each liferaft can be got to the lifelines within 10 seconds.
11.4.2	Liferaft(s) representing 50 percent crew capacity (not counting overload) shall be stowed below decks, in special stowage(s) containing liferaft(s) only, from which each liferaft can be got to the lifelines within 30 seconds.
11.4.3	Each liferaft must have its emergency painter permanently secured to suitable strongpoints.
11.4.4	Each liferaft must be designed, built and equipped in accordance with the Safety of Life at Sea (SOLAS) Convention of 17 June 1960, Chapter III, Regulations 15 and 17(a).
11.4.5	Each liferaft must be marked with the sail number of the yacht so as to be visible from the air.
11.4.6	Each liferaft must have been inspected, tested and approved within six months of the start of the race from London, and within two months of the start of the race from Sydney by the manufacturer or other competent authority and yachts must carry on board the certificates issued by such authority stating that the raft is approved for service. The certificate shall also state the manner in which the raft should be stowed, i.e. horizontally or vertically, and (b) the list of contents of the raft package.
11.5	*Emergency kits to accompany liferafts*
	Two holdalls or bags of canvas or similar material, each having the following:
11.5.1	A strong simple fastening unaffected by seawater;
11.5.2	8 feet (2.5 m) floating line, permanently fitted;
11.5.3	bright colour;
11.5.4	positive buoyancy when packed;
11.5.5	each holdall or bag must be kept in a special stowage from which it can be got to the lifelines within 30 seconds;
11.5.6	each kit must contain the following items in individual watertight packages:

(a) Clothing for warmth and protection;
(b) waterproof torch suitable for signalling (as specified in 8.4), with spare batteries;
(c) pyrotechnic distress signals (may form part of the total required in 11.8–11.8.4);

(d) two dye markers;

(e) water in unbreakable, re-sealable bottles, and one or more solar stills to be used in emergency only;

(f) emergency food rations and vitamin tablets;

(g) sunburn lotion;

(h) shark repellant.

11.6   At least one horseshoe type life ring equipped with a self-igniting high-intensity water light, a whistle and a drogue within reach of the helmsman and ready for instant use.

11.7   At least one more horseshoe type life ring equipped with a whistle, dye marker, drogue, a high-intensity waterproof light, and a pole and flag. The pole is to be attached to the ring with 25 feet (8 m) of floating line and is to be of a length and so ballasted that the flag will fly at least 8 feet (2.45 m) off the water.

11.7.1   A second set of equipment as required in 11.7 shall be held in reserve.

11.8   Pyrotechnic distress signals stowed in waterproof containers:

11.8.1   Twelve red parachute flares;

11.8.2   Six long-duration smoke flares;

11.8.3   Twelve red hand flares;

11.8.4   Twelve white hand flares.

11.9   Heaving line (50 foot (16 m) minimum length, floating line) readily accessible to cockpit.

2 Recommended Courses

These extracts from *Ocean Passages for the World* are reprinted with the permission of the Controller of Her Majesty's Stationery Office. They detail dangers *en route*, and give advice on what courses a prudent sailing ship should take.

OUTWARD LONDON TO SYDNEY

Route 1,007: Channel to Arquipélago de Cabo Verde (Cape Verde Islands)

On leaving the English Channel at once make westing, as the prevailing winds are from that direction. With a fair wind from the Lizard, steer a west-south-westerly course to gain an offing in long. 10° or 12°W.

If the wind should be from the westward keep on the tack which enables most westing to be made to get a good offing, and keep clear of the Bay of Biscay, even standing to the north-westward until well able to weather Cabo Finisterre on the starboard tack. By making a long board to the westward nothing is lost, as the wind will generally be found to veer, so that a change of wind will be favourable, and even permit a vessel to pursue a course with a free wind; whilst if embayed in the Bay of Biscay, and change of wind to the westward would necessitate beating to windward against the current.

It must be borne in mind that the prevailing winds and currents have a tendency to set towards Ushant, and into the Bay of Biscay when southward of it. To get well to the westward is therefore of the greatest importance. Ushant should, in no case, be sighted.

From long. 10° or 12°W., shape course to pass Madeira at any convenient distance, giving a wide berth to Cabo Finisterre, in passing it, as the current from the Atlantic usually sets right on-shore there. In the winter months it is preferable to pass westward of Madeira, for the strong westerly gales which occur in November, December and January produce eddy winds and heavy squalls eastward of the island.

From Madeira the best track is to pass to the westward and just in sight of Arquipélago de Cabo Verde (Cape Verde Islands) as the winds are stronger and steadier to the westward than to the eastward of them.

Arquipélago de Cabo Verde to the Equator

In considering where to cross the equator it is necessary to bear in mind that if a vessel crosses far to the westward there will be less interval of Doldrum to cross, but it may be requisite to tack to weather the coast of South America, and these crossings vary during the year, as the direction of the south-east trade wind is more southerly when the sun is north of the equator than when south.

After passing the Arquipélago de C. Verde, stand to the southward between the meridians of 26° and 29°W., being nearer 26°W. from May to October, and nearer 29°W. from November to April. The equator should be crossed at points varying according to the season of the year, as follows:

In July, August and September, the southerly winds will be met with between 10° and 12°N. On meeting them steer on the starboard tack so as to cross lat. 5°N. between 17° and 19°W. Go round then on the other tack, and cross the equator, as in May and June, between 25° and 23°W.

In October, November and December, the southerly winds will be met with between lat. 8° and 6°N. On meeting them, steer so as to cross lat. 5°N between 20° and 23°W., then take the tack which gives most southing, and cross the equator between 29° and 24°W.

CAUTION: The South Equatorial current is not so strong in the northern winter as in the summer and autumn months; but the mariner must remember that the strength of the current increases as it advances towards the American coast.

Equator to Cape Town and the Cape of Good Hope

Having crossed the equator as recommended, stand across the south-east trade wind on the port tack, even should the vessel fall off to W. by S., for the wind will draw more to the eastward as the vessel advances, and finally to East at the southern limit of the trade. When in the vicinity of St Paul rocks, frequent astronomical observations should be made, the current watched and allowed for, and a good lookout kept, as these rocks are steep-to, and can only be seen on a clear day from a distance of 8 miles. The same precautions are necessary if passing westward of Arquipélago de Fernando de Noronha, when approaching the dangerous Atol das Rocas, on which a light was established in 1882. It was customary, in proceeding to the southward in the south-east trade, to sight Ilha da Trindade (Lat. 20° 30′S., Long. 29° 19′ W.) to test the rate of their chronometers, and to take a fresh departure; but this has become increasingly unnecessary owing to the availability of radio time signals. During the greater part of the year the south-east trade fails on a line drawn from the Cape of Good Hope to Ilhas da Trindade and Martin Vaz. This limit varies from 3°, according to the position of the sun.

When to the southward of the south-east trade, fresh winds variable in direction will be met. Those from north-east through north to north-west, if accompanied by cloudy weather, often shift suddenly to south-west of south, but sometimes the wind steadies between west and west-south-west. From Ilha da Trindade shape course to the south-eastward to cross the parallel of 30°S., in about long.

22°W., and the meridian of Greenwich in about lat. 35°–37°S., whence, to the Cape of Good Hope, winds from the westward and southward usually prevail. If bound eastward round the Cape of Good Hope, cross the meridian of Greenwich in about lat. 40°S.

Cape Town or Cape of Good Hope to ports in Australia and New Zealand

Vessels bound to Australian ports would make the passage at about the parallel of 39° or 40°S. but those bound to Tasmania or New Zealand, would do so at between 42° or 43° S., especially from October to March, the summer months. Between 39°S. and 43°S. the winds generally blow from some western point, and seldom with more strength than will admit of carrying sail. In a higher latitude the weather is frequently more boisterous and stormy; sudden changes of wind with squally wet weather are almost constantly to be expected, especially in the winter season. Île Amsterdam may be seen from a distance of 60 miles in clear weather.

In summer, many vessels take a more southern route, some going as far south as the parallel of 52°S. latitude, but the steadiness and comparatively moderate strength of the winds, with the smoother seas and more genial climate north of 40°S., compensate by comfort and security for the time presumed to be saved by taking a shorter route. Tempestuous gales, sudden violent and fitful shifts of wind, accompanied by hail or snow, and terrific and irregular seas are often encountered in the higher latitudes; moreover the islands in the higher latitudes are so frequently shrouded in fog that often the first sign of their vicinity is the sound of the surf beating against them.

CAUTION: Ice. South-eastward of the Cape of Good Hope, midway between Kerguelen island and the meridian of Cape Leeuwin, midway between New Zealand and Cabo de Hornos (Cape Horn), and north-eastward of Cabo de Hornos, icebergs are most numerous. The periods of maximum and minimum frequency vary greatly. It may happen that while ships are passing ice in lower latitudes, others, in higher latitudes, find the ocean free of ice.

The lengths of many of the Southern Ocean icebergs are remarkable; bergs of 5 to 20 miles in length are frequently sighted south of the 40th parallel, and bergs of from 20 to 50 miles in length are far from uncommon.

It may be gathered from numerous observations that bergs may, in places, be fallen in with anywhere south of the 30th parallel, that as many as 4,500 bergs have been observed in a run of 2,000 miles, that estimated heights of 800 to 1,700 feet (243 m to 518 m) are not uncommon, and that bergs of from 6 to 82 miles in length are numerous.

Approach to Bass Strait

(i) North of King Island (recommended). In approaching Bass Strait to make the land at Moonlight head or the light at Cape Otway, the currents must be carefully attended to, particularly during south-westerly or southerly winds; vessels have been wrecked on King Island by not steering for Cape Otway. When approaching Bass Strait in thick weather, or when uncertain of the vessel's position, do not reduce the soundings to less than 40 fathoms (73 m). Soundings of 60 to 70 fathoms (109 m or 128 m) will be found at 25 or 30 miles westward of King Island. Outside this limit the soundings deepen rapidly to over 100 fathoms (182 m).

The high bold promontory of Cape Otway is easily distinguished by the white lighthouse on it, and by the signal station, to which all passing vessels are recommended to show their number. It is desirable to round Cape Otway at a distance of not less than 3 or 4 miles.

CAUTION: In approaching King Island from the westward, especially during thick or hazy weather, caution is required on account of the variable strength of the current, which sets to the south-east with a force varying from a half to 2 knots, according to the strength and duration of the westerly winds, and sounding is recommended.

(ii) South of King Island (not recommended)

To Sydney

After reaching the longitude of Australia, there is a summer and a winter route as follows:
Summer route: leave the main route across the Indian Ocean at about the 120th meridian E. and steer to pass round the south of Tasmania.

After rounding South Cape, give a berth of 20 or 30 miles to Cape Pillar and the east coast of Tasmania, to escape the baffling winds and calms which frequently perplex vessels inshore, while a steady breeze is blowing in the offing. This is more desirable from December to March, when easterly winds prevail, and a current is said to be experienced off the south-east coast at 20 to 60 miles from the shore, running northward at the rate of three-quarters of a knot, while inshore it is running in the opposite direction with nearly double that rate. From a position about 30 miles eastward of Cape Pillar, proceed on a course of about 012° for about 350 miles to a position 15 miles eastward of Cape Howe, whence continue as directly as possible to make Sydney, but keeping at first at a distance from the coast in order to lessen the strength of the south-going Australian coast current, not closing the land till northward of South Head, Port Jackson.

Some navigators prefer to stand eastward into long. 155°E., before turning northward for Port Jackson, and thus escape almost altogether the southerly set.

HOMEWARD PASSAGE SYDNEY TO LONDON

Route 1,260: Sydney to Cabo de Hornos (Cape Horn)
At all seasons and from whatever quarter the wind may blow, it is advisable on

leaving Port Jackson to proceed to the southward rather than to the northward of New Zealand. Advantage therefore should be taken of the most favourable winds for either reaching the position in about lat. 48° 30′S., between the Snares and Auckland isles, to join Route 1,251 (a) or, if baffled by southerly winds and favoured by fine weather, the passage through Cook strait may be taken with advantage, especially from October to February, joining Route 1,270 (2) from Wellington off that port.

See also Route 1,251 (b) for an alternative route if passing southward of New Zealand.

Route 1,251: Main route across the Southern Ocean to Cabo de Hornos (Cape Horn)

The main route across the Southern Ocean from the Cape of Good Hope (see Route 1,091(7) (a)) passes southward of Tasmania, in about long. 147°E., between the parallels of 45°S. and 47°S. From this position a vessel should proceed by one of the following routes:

(a) Usual route. All seasons. Pass round the south end of New Zealand in about lat. 48° 30′S., clear of The Snares (Lat. 48° 01′S., Long. 166° 36′E.). From this point steer to the eastward between Bounty Islands (Lat. 47° 41′S., Long. 179° 03′E.) and Antipodes Islands (Lat. 49° 40′S., Long. 178° 50′E.), whence, inclining slightly to the southward, the route assumes, as a mean track, the parallel of 51°S. from the meridian of 150°W., across the ocean to long. 120°W.; keeping at about 60 miles northward of this parallel from December to February (so as to be more clear of ice), and at 60 miles to the southward of it from June to August; but in this case, also, dependent on ice conditions. (See Note under (b), below.) From the meridian of 115°W., incline gradually to the southward, to round Islas Diego Ramirez and Cabo de Hornos (Cape Horn) (see Routes 1,375, 1,040† and 1,083 to 1,087, inclusive).

(b) Alternative route. Summer only. Some navigators take, during the summer months (December to February), a more southerly route from the position southward of Tasmania, so as to pass between Auckland islands and Campbell island in about lat. 52°S., and make the passage across the Pacific Ocean in between lat. 54° and 55°S.

This course would, with a sea clear of ice, and favourable weather, doubtless ensure the quickest passage, as being the shorter distance, but experience has proved that at nearly all seasons of the year so much time is lost at night and in thick weather, and even serious danger incurred on account of the great quantities of ice met with in these higher latitudes, that a parallel even as far north as 47° has been adopted with advantage. Between this latter parallel and that of 50°, it is believed the mariner will experience steadier winds, smoother water, absence of ice, and will probably make as short a passage, and certainly one in a more genial climate, and with more security, than in a higher latitude.

Note: the seaman in navigating this wide expanse of ocean, and also for rounding

Cabo de Hornos, should be provided with the Ice Chart of the Southern Hemisphere, No. 1,241, published by the Admiralty, wherein he will find much useful information.

Route 1,375: Rounding Cape Horn

Make as direct a course as possible to round Cabo de Hornos closely in the summer months (from September to February), but 60 to 80 miles to the southward of it in the winter months. See Route 1,083(1) for directions for rounding Cabo de Hornos.

Note: fogs. These are rare on the coast of Tierra del Fuego and in the vicinity of Cabo de Hornos (Cape Horn), but thick rainy weather prevails, with strong winds, the sky even in moderate weather being generally overcast and cloudy; a clear day is a rare occurrence.

Route 1,401

The summer months, December and January, are the best for making a passage from the Pacific to the Atlantic, though the passage is so short and easy that it hardly requires a choice of time. See also Route 1,083(1). A summary of the routes onward from Cabo de Hornos is given under Route 1,375.

Note: making the land after rounding Cabo de Hornos. The best way is to make the land westward of Cabo San Diego, in Tierra del Fuego, where the shore is free from outlying dangers. While a southwest gale is blowing the vessel can 'lie-to' under easy sail in smooth water, and when the wind shifts to the north-west a good run may be made before the wind is again to the southwest. In the Estrecho de le Maire it is better to keep mid-channel, the overfalls off Cabo San Diego being very heavy at times. A vessel drifting from Cabo de Hornos towards Isla de los Estados (Staten island) in a southwest gale should run boldly through Estrecho de le Maire, haul up under the land of Tierra del Fuego, and wait for a shift of wind.

Anchorage: temporary anchorage is available in Bahia Buen Suceso (Good Success bay), about 9 miles southward of Cabo San Diego.

Route 1,083: Cabo de Hornos (Cape Horn) to the Channel
(1) From the Pacific to the Atlantic round Cabo de Hornos

Rounding the Horn from west to east is a comparatively easy matter, for the prevailing winds are favourable and the current sets strongly to the eastward as Cabo de Hornos itself is approached. The passage is usually made between lats. 56° and 57°S. to the northward of the route from the Atlantic Ocean to the Pacific Ocean (see Route 1,007(8)); the current does not run strongly at 50 miles southward from Cabo de Hornos. December and January are the most favourable months; June and July, when easterly winds are not unusual, are the least favourable. August and September are months in which heavy westerly gales may be expected, with snow and hail.

See also Route 1,401 and Note under the same; and also, regarding fog, under Route 1,375.

(2) *From Cabo de Hornos to the Equator*

(a) Usual route. The usual route is to pass about 80 miles southward of the Falkland Islands, and to make for a central point in about lat. 35°S., long. 30°W., but to the westward of it between April and August, or to the eastward of it from September to March. From this point there are two routes northward, according to season, as follows:

(i) April to August. Stand northward to the intersection of lat. 10°S. with long. 25°W., keeping as much as possible to the westward of that meridian throughout, and cross the equator between 25° and 28°W. It might even be possible to pass between Cabo Frio and Ilha da Trindade at this time of year.

(ii) September to March. From the position in lat. 35°S. stand on to the north-north-eastward to about long. 20°W. and lat. 25°S., and then run northward with the south-east trade wind, and cross the equator between longs. 22° and 25°W.

(b) Alternative routes consequent on ice conditions. There are three alternative routes (i), (ii), and (iii) below, if ice is seen to be prevalent; they are particularly suitable to the months between October and February.

Ice may be met with eastward of Cabo de Hornos and the Falkland Islands at all times of the year, but is more common between October and February, which are the most favourable months for rounding Cabo de Hornos, as stated in (1) above.

The mean ice limit for this region trends north-eastwards from Cabo de Hornos, through lat. 50°S., long. 52°W., as far as lat. 40°S., long. 35°W., but icebergs have been met with as far west at the Falklands; northward of 40°S. they are rare, but a good look-out should still be kept for them.

Numerous icebergs and extensive icefields have also been seen at different times in the space south-eastward of the above limit. Some of these icebergs have exceeded 20 miles in length, and were very numerous in 1892, 1893, and 1894. In 1906 numerous icebergs were seen north-westward of the above limit; in long. about 56° 30′W. they extended from lat 50° to 45° 30′S.

Icebergs should, if possible, be passed to windward to avoid the loose ice floating to leeward.

(i) After rounding Cabo de Hornos steer so as to cross the parallel of 50°S. in about long. 51°W., and the parallel of 40°S. in about long. 45°W., and then make northing until the south-east trade is met; joining with Route 1,078 (b) from Rio de la Plata (October to April) at about lat. 35°S.

(ii) Some navigators recommend the following route. From October to February, pass westward of the Falkland Islands, on account of the greater freedom from ice then, in that region, and then stand to the north-eastward, joining with alternative route (i) at lat. 35°S. in about long. 41°W.

(iii) If unable to pass west of the Falkland Islands, pass as close to the eastward as the wind will allow, and thence as above.

CAUTION: If meeting with a foul wind, whilst to the southward of 40°S., it would be better to stand to the north-westward than to the eastward, as ice is likely to be encountered not far to the eastward of the Falkland Islands.

(3) From the Equator to the Channel

Follow Route 1,044 (i) Cape Town to the Channel, which joins the route from Cabo de Hornos at the Equator. From April to August keep on the western side of the northward track, and from September to March on the eastern side.

Route 1,044: To the Channel

First obtain a good offing to the north-westward, as squalls from the north-west and west-north-west are not infrequent near the coast, and have been experienced in both seasons. Then shape course for St Helena (Lat. 15° 55′S., Long. 5° 42′W.): in cloudy weather get on its parallel some distance to the eastward, to avoid missing it, if intending to call there.

From St Helena steer a direct course for Ascension, passing it on either side, and crossing the equator between long. 25° and 30°W. (in July between long. 20° and 25°W. to ensure better winds). Then make a northerly course to reach the north-east trade as soon as possible (in July and August crossing lat. 10°N. west of long. 30°W.) and run through it. The trade wind will probably be lost in about lat. 26° to 28°N., and from long. 38° to 40°W., when westerly winds may be expected, and on reaching these shape course for the English Channel.

Notes: It is seldom advisable to pass eastward of the Arquipélago dos Açôres (Azores), but should the wind draw to the north-west when near them the most convenient channel thorough them may be taken. If easterly winds are experienced after passing the Arquipélago dos Açôres the vessel should still be kept on the starboard tack, as westerly winds will probably be sooner found.

From November to February, a vessel should pass about 50 miles westward of Ilha das Flores and Ilha do Corvo; but from June to August, at about 250 miles westward of these islands. At other times of the year, at intermediate positions.

3 The Yachts and Their Crews

Anaconda II, the all-Australian entry in the Clipper Race, was the largest yacht to take part, though not the most heavily penalized on handicap because of the measurement of her rig and hull compared with *Great Britain II*. She was designed by the British naval architect Alan Buchanan and built at a Naval yard in Adelaide, South Australia. Economic worries forced her owner Josko Grubic to keep building cost low but she was by no means cheap. Built from glass-reinforced plastic, the hull was designed to the International Offshore Ruling with an eye to the demands of long-distance racing in the roughest seas and special hull strength in the form of longitudinal stringers was a major feature.

The accident at her launching, which injured her owner, prevented the yacht sailing in the first leg from London to Sydney.

Of the five yachts that sailed from Sydney on the second leg *Anaconda* was certainly the most comfortable below decks and carried the most sophisticated navigation equipment, though much of the benefit from this equipment and comfort was lost with the main source of electricity early in the race. Some observers thought that her rig was too light and that her sail wardrobe was too small, but, apart from a broken inner forestay when off New Zealand in the storms that cost the French their rudder and the Italians a knockdown, she stood the voyage well.

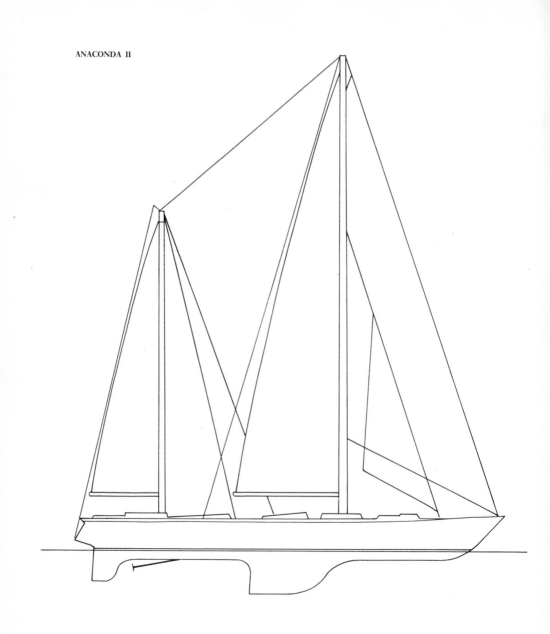

Crew list

Name	Age	Nationality	Leg sailed	Comments
Josko Grubic	51	Australian	2	Skipper/owner. Owns Adelaide-based company, Trans Line Freighters, and two properties in South Australia.
Charles Wall-Smith	40s	Australian	2	Butcher, well known in yachting circles in South Australia as 'Chook-Fireball-Wall-Hurricane-Smith'. First mate.
Martin Carney	28	Australian	2	Clerk.
Nic Creech	27	Australian	2	Journalist. One of the most experienced crew members, been around Sydney sailing circuit for years.
Lou Davidson	38	Australian	2	Navigator. Just retired from Royal Australian Navy as hydrographer.
Paul Howard	29	British	2	Builder. Provided *Anaconda* with emergency radio. Attended night navigational school. Flew out from London especially to crew *Anaconda*.
Douglas Justins	28	Australian	2	Medical practitioner. *Anaconda*'s doctor.
Craig Mitchell	30	Australian	2	Physiotherapist.
Hans Savimaki	27	Australian	2	Sugar farmer.
Roger Scales	29	Australian	2	Company director.
John Taylor	20	Australian	2	Student, very keen experienced yachtsman.
Owen Trewartha	54	Australian	2	Linotype operator.
Arthur Vandenbroek	27	Australian	2	Motor trimmer, working as sail maker on board.

This yacht, with her schooner rig, was already proven both as a design and as individually, a good easily managed seaboat. She is a sistership to Andre Viant's *Grand Louis*, a totally unsponsored and successful entry in the Whitbread race, but Malingri's preparations had gone further than merely the study of designs of other yachts. Apart from the transatlantic race, the yacht had been at sea for more than a year prior to the start of the Clipper Race, competing in races in the Mediterranean before leaving for the United States. The yacht, built of glass fibre to the design of Dominique Presles, was entered with the full knowledge that the main prize for line honours in the Clipper Race would not be theirs. The crew entered with the real feeling that sailing comes first, and prizes, rules and other paraphernalia were not as important as making the full distance for the pleasure of being at sea.

Crew list

Name	Age	Nationality	Leg sailed	Comments
Dionigi Malingri di Bagnolo	37	Italian	1 and 2	Company director. Sailed Whitbread race. Skipper.
Geoffrey Cross	31	British	1 and 2	School teacher. Radio operator.
Antonio Giovannini		Italian	1 and 2	Student.
Daniele Legler		Italian	1 and 2	Actor.
Luigi Manzi		Italian	1 and 2	Student.
Paolo Mascheroni		Italian	1 only	
Claudio Stampi	22	Brazilian, lives in Italy	1 only	Student.
Gilles Varillon	20	French	1 only	Had very little sailing experience, sailed London–Sydney with *CS e RB II*, Sydney–London with *Kriter II*.
Elnora Waring	29	British, lives in Italy	1 and 2	Professional model, photographer, yogi.

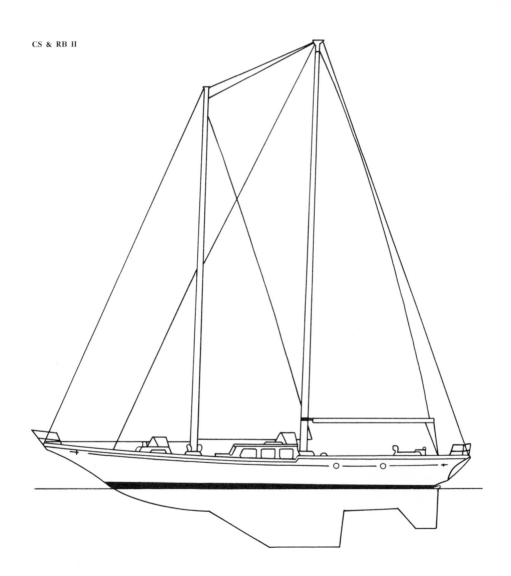

Great Britain II started on the *Financial Times* Clipper Race with one circumnavigation of the globe already under her keel. She was designed as a 'one-off'
yacht by the New York-based British yacht designer Alan Gurney for Chay Blyth
specifically for the 1973–4 Whitbread race around the world, line honours being
the criterion, though the main handicap prize was also in the minds of her
skipper and crew. She collected nine trophies in the Whitbread race, including
line honours for the last two stages from Sydney to Rio and from Rio home to
Portsmouth. Her design had already been proved as she was based on Bob
Johnson's ketch *Windward Passage*; comparison of the two yachts was possible
for the first time during the Clipper Race when they were in Sydney at the same
time. She was built by Derek Kelsall, perhaps better known for his construction
of multi-hulled yachts, using the sandwich foam method which produced a good
strength-to-weight ratio. Her 77-foot overall length, 68-foot waterline and 9-foot
draft give her a total displacement of 70,000 lbs and she carries a sail area of
2,500 feet on the wind, but of course, several spinnakers capable of more than
doubling this when running. She carried a crew of fourteen on the outward leg to
Australia, and sixteen on the way home. Below decks she is spartan but designed
for total practicability rather than comfort; in rough weather the more basic the
accommodation the easier life becomes below decks.

The condition of the hull and rigging of the yacht after both legs of the Clipper
Race was, to the spectator, remarkable, though some structural problems seemed
to have been inherited from her earlier voyage. These, it appeared, were caused
by leaks below the engine mounts aft of the keel, probably due to the pressure
exerted by the backstay tensioner combining with downpressure on the mast to
the keel as well as working by the hull aft of the keel. These problems were easily
solved and within weeks of completing the Clipper Race the yacht was taken over
by boys from the London Sailing Project to compete in the transatlantic tall-
ships race, organized by the Sail Training Association as part of the American
Independence bicentenary celebrations.

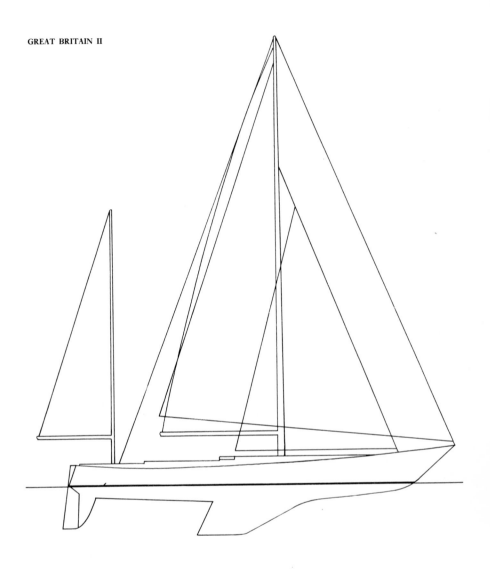

Mike Gill	Skipper	Team Manager. Took part in Whitbread race as Navigator of *British Soldier* on the Sydney to Rio leg. Captain in Royal Engineers.
Dave Leslie	Chief Mate	Staff Sergeant Technician in Royal Electrical and Mechanical Engineers. Bosun of Yacht during period prior to race. On *British Soldier* for leg 4 of Whitbread race.
John Bagnall	Navigator & Mate	Project Director, late Royal Artillery. Retired two days before the race started (36 years service).
Mike Summerfield	Mate & Bosun	Captain in Welsh Guards. Has skippered the Household Brigade yacht *Gladeye*.
Ian Kirkwood	Photographer	A competent diver as well as having sailing experience in UK waters. Captain Royal Corps of Transport.
Colin Wagstaff	Mate & Purser	Captain in Worcestershire and Sherwood Foresters Regt. Owns his own boat and joined the project as Administrator.
Richard Old	Engineer	Corporal in Royal Scots Dragoon Guards. Had considerable experience teaching members of his Regt to sail.
Parfoot	Winchman & Medical Assistant	Chief Petty Officer. Medical Tech at Royal Naval Hospital, Haslar, Gosport.
Keith Powell	Radio Operator	Royal Marines. Stationed at Poole.
Martin Bevan	Electrician	Lieutenant in Royal Signals. Considerable experience in Coastal Sailing and sailed as Watch Officer with the London Sailing Project.
Dennis Cooke	Sail mender	Leading Airman in Royal Navy. Stationed at RAF Lossiemouth. Expert in maintaining and repairing Safety Equipment.
John Mclean	Sail mender & radio op.	Captain, Royal Signals.
Tony Waldron	Sail Mender	Staff Sergeant, Royal Australian Survey Regt. Australian Services representative for Leg 1.
Tom Balch		Corporal in Royal Corps of Transport. Took part in the 1974 Tall Ships Race on HMSTY *Sabre*.

Roy Mullender	Skipper	C.P.O., Royal Navy.
Billy King-Harman	Mate	Captain, Royal Artillery, at time serving in BAOR. Took part in Whitbread race, as crew member on *Second Life*.
Jim Hollingsworth	Rigger	Captain, Royal Artillery, from Army Apprentices College, Arborfield. Had considerable coastal experience and had taken part in several training cruises. Home town: Stoke on Trent.
Dave Leslie	Chief Mate	The only member of the *GB II* project to take part in both legs of the race. Staff Sergeant Technician in Royal Electrical and Mechanical Engineers. Bosun of Yacht during period prior to race. On *British Soldier* for leg 4 of Whitbread race. Home town: Bainsford, Falkirk.
John Langhorne	Winchman/ Purser	Major, in Queens Division, considerable coastal experience and took part in the 1975 Tall Ships Race on HMSTY *Sabre*.
Phil Shephard	Engineer/ Electrician	Lance Corporal REME, an experienced electrician who carried out a great deal of work on the boat during the refit. Had a good background of coastal experience. Home town: Farnborough, Hants.
Ian Parrotte	Cameraman	Sergeant, Royal Army Ordnance Corps. Extensive experience cruising in Baltic and UK waters. Clerk of *GB II* project. Home town: Birmingham.
Peter Enzer	Sailmaker	Captain in the Royal Engineers, serving in Washington satellite tracking team. Considerable racing experience in English Channel.
Bob Dickens	Winchman	Royal Marine Instructor at Towyn Outward Bound School.
Tom Snook	Sailmaker	Sergeant in the RAF based at St Athan, an air-frame fitter and therefore conversant with spar mending.
Dick Counter	Doctor	Squadron Leader, RAF. Qualified surgeon, Medical cover for Leg 2.
Bill Porter	Mate	C.P.O., R.N.
Chris Windley	Sparman/ Sailmaker	Able Seaman, R.N.
Brian Haydon	Winchman	Captain, Australian Army
Keith Powell	Radio operator	Royal Marine: stationed at Poole.
Bob Bell	Rigger	Petty Officer, Royal Navy.

This little yacht, a 55-foot welded steel ketch, fell somewhere between a comfortable family cruising yacht, a miniature ice breaker and the embodied shape of tenacity. If the crew of *CS e RB II* knew before the start that they had little or no chance of line honours, then the crew of *The Great Escape* mush have known with almost equal certainty that the back marker's place was to be for them for most of the voyage. A standard production Trewes 56, *The Great Escape* belied her size, for below decks she was as carefully planned as any Dutch ship and embodied many features one finds in far larger vessels; a large day cabin aft, with well-finished woodwork, a spacious galley area, and small but adequate cabins providing berths for all the crew. On deck the solidity of the yacht was maintained with stout rigging, a deckhouse with windows that only finally cracked when the protective screens were fitted in storms in the southern oceans, and guard rails that would have done credit to a tug. There was a shop aboard that was opened once every week for the purchase of essential needs, cigarettes, sweets, toothpaste and soap for example; and a continuing feeling of well-being that even the most unpleasant storms scarcely dented. Slow because of the weight-to-sail area ratio in light weather, the yacht could sail to her designed hull maximum speed in the heavier following winds. Her average speed for the entire voyage was about 150 miles per day. The only serious structural problem was the working of the bearing in the rudder stock which caused a little worry aboard when the crew heard successive thumping as the rudder shifted a few millimetres from side to side in heavy following seas. A remarkable little craft sailed by a remarkable crew of tenacious people.

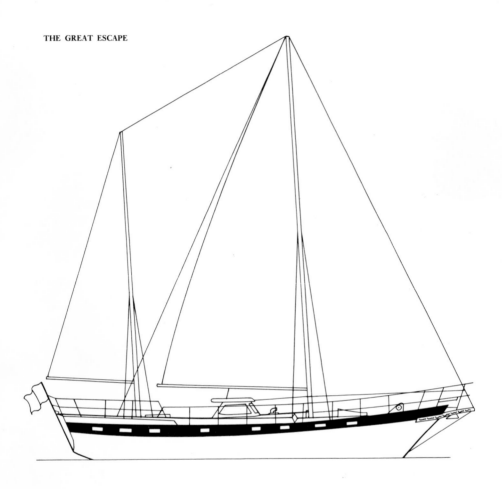

Crew list

Name	Age	Nationality	Leg sailed	Comments
Henk Huisman	50	Dutch	1	Skipper Leg 1 only. Owner of *The Great Escape* and Watersports Twellegea.
Dirk Nauta	32	Dutch	2	Skipper leg 2. Professional skipper with Watersports Uitwellingerga.
Jan Carree	31	Dutch	1 and 2	Architect.
Bart-Jan van Cronenburg	33	Dutch	1 and 2	Analyst.
Jose Detmers	27	Dutch	1 and 2	Nurse.
Elly Donker	41	Dutch	1 and 2	Female.
Freek Faber	35	Dutch	1 and 2	Metal worker.
Paul Fennis	26	Dutch	1 and 2	Computer operater.
Rob Kwekkeboom	30	Dutch	2	Nutrition specialist.
Hans Otto Luneburg	36	German	1	Sailor.
Henk Meester	23	Dutch	1 and 2	Photo-lithographer.
Sjerp Noorda	41	Dutch	1 and 2	Merchant.
Jacobus Olie	18	Dutch	2	
Joost Reedijk	18	Dutch	1 and 2	Sails rigger.
Sjoerd Rotmans	24	Dutch	2	Social worker.
Raymond Weber	22	Swiss	1 and 2	Draughtsman.
Ruedi Zimmerman	29	Swiss	1	Student of social science.

Kriter II was no newcomer to the business of racing over long distances when she went to the starting line off Sheerness at the end of August 1975, although many might not have recognized her in her new French guise and colours. She was built for Leslie Williams and his partner Alan Smith in Poole to the design of John Sharp in 1973. She was originally named, for the Whitbread race, *Windward Spirit*, but then during financial problems which resulted in successful legal action by her owners, her name was changed to *Burton Cutter* as an acknowledgement of help received from sponsors. Destined for the charter business after completing the Whitbread race around the world, she was scarcely ready to sail when she left Portsmouth for Cape Town, but she took line honours into Cape Town only to be forced out of the race in the early stages of the second leg with severe hull weaknesses. She then raced to Rio de Janeiro from South Africa and rejoined the Whitbread fleet for the final leg home.

In 1974 she took mono-hull line honours in the *Observer* race around Britain and then reverted to charter until her owners and their agents Castlemain Marine were approached by Michel Etevenon, representing Patriarche and Kriter wines.

The rest of her tale has now been told.

Extensively and hurriedly refitted and strengthened by the French at Lymington, her aluminium hull is longer and heavier than *Great Britain II* though the waterline length of the two yachts is identical. Her foresail area was, for the Clipper Race, a little less at 1,040 square feet, as was her mainsail at 756 square feet, though her mizzen mast was taller and therefore the area of this sail and the potential area of mizzen staysails larger. Extensive alterations to her deck layout altered her appearance, but despite these differences she claimed only hours from *Great Britain II* on handicap for the full distance around the world.

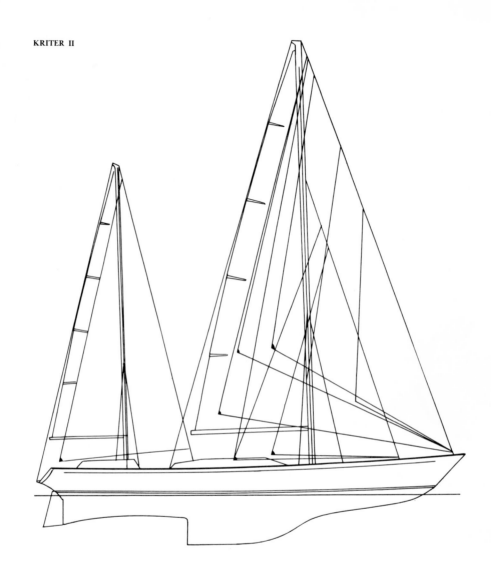

Crew list

Name	Age	Nationality	Leg sailed	Comments
Olivier de Kersauson de Pennendreff		French	1 and 2	Skipper. Professional sailor.
Georges Commarmond	32	French	1 and 2	Bosun–cook. Designer.
Yves Olivaux		French	1 and 2	Navigator. Retired Air France captain.
Jacques Arestan	22	French	1 and 2	Student of business studies.
François Boivin	28	French	1 and 2	Doctor.
François Boucher	20	French	1 and 2	Student of business studies.
Daniel Gilard	26	French	1 and 2	Maritime consultant.
Julian Gildersleeve	23	British	1 and 2	Charter skipper.
Pascal Guillemet	21	French	1 and 2	Student of aeronautical and motor technology.
Vincent de Kerviler	24	French	1 and 2	Student of economics and marketing.
Alain Labbe	23	French	1 and 2	Student.
Patrick Meulemeester	23	French	1	Student.
Bruno de la Sablière	22	French	1 and 2	Marketing student.
Christophe White *dit* Smith	22	French	1 and 2	Journalist and radio reporter.
Gilles Varillon	20	French	2	

4 Comparison of Daily Positions

So that their progress can be compared *Patriarch*'s dates have been adjusted to those which would have followed from her leaving for Australia on 1 September 1869: she left in fact on 3 December.

Great Britain II			Patriarch		
31 August	51.20N	00.50E	1 September	48.27N	6.50W
1 September	50.10N	01.14W	2	44.58N	12.45W
2	49.08N	03.48W	3	40.33N	15.48W
3	48.17N	05.45W	4	38.11N	16.48W
4	45.10N	10.12W	5	34.45N	17.25W
5	44.03N	12.10W	6	33.15N	18.4 W
6	41.12N	13.10W	7	31.28N	19.8 W
7	37.59N	14.25W	8	28.53N	20.58W
8	34.46N	16.18W	9	26.30N	22.26W
9	32.10N	18.40W	10	23.40N	24.32W
10	29.03N	20.22W	11	20.12N	27.7 W
11	25.15N	22.58W	12	16.2 N	27.32W
12	21.49N	22.24W	13	12.31N	27.15W
13	17.55N	23.30W	14	8.43N	26.59W
14	14.52N	23.55W	15	6.15N	26.59W
15	13.39N	24.27W	16	5.12N	26.50W
16	10.55N	23.20W	17	4.8 N	27.7 W
17	07.48N	22.11W	18	1.10N	27.57W
18	05.02N	21.55W	19	1.54S	29.57W
19	04.05N	22.05W	20	5.3 S	31.19W
20	01.51N	23.01W	21	9.19S	31.44W
21	00.09N	22.23W	22	13.21S	31.15W
22	03.00S	22.15W	23	16.43S	30.58W
23	06.44S	22.06W	24	18.19S	30.42W
24	10.18S	22.21W	25	20.16S	30.2 W
25	13.42S	22.20W	26	21.58S	29.32W
26	17.02S	21.40W	27	23.35S	28.47W
27	19.04S	21.47W	28	24.58S	27.44W
28	20.31S	19.47W	29	26.8 S	28.58W
29	21.29S	17.28W	30	28.23S	24.43W
30	24.39S	17.10W	1 October	31.18S	21.37W
1 October	27.34S	15.36W	2	33.16S	18.53W
2	30.48S	13.00W	3	34.9 S	18.18W

Date	Lat	Long		Date	Lat	Long
3	33.22S	09.19W		4	35.45S	14.34W
4	35.37S	04.56W		5	36.45S	11.45W
5	36.54S	00.05E		6	35.50S	8.21W
6	38.21S	05.00E		7	35.45S	7.18W
7	39.56S	10.06E		8	38.81S	2.31W
8	41.44S	15.50E		9	40.11S	1.5 E
9	42.06S	21.30E		10	41 S	4.12E
10	42.14S	20.09E		11	42.16S	9.40E
11	42.50S	31.55E		12	43.25S	14.8 E
12	43.33S	37.17E		13	44.42S	19.18E
13	43.31S	43.19E		14	45.15S	23.48E
14	43.22S	47.24E		15	45.33S	28.58E
15	43.06S	52.14E		16	45.40S	30.47E
16	42.37S	56.53E		17	45.41S	34.23E
17	43.48S	61.55E		18	45.59S	39.37E
18	44.58S	67.46E		19	46.25S	45.50E
19	45.17S	71.10E		20	48.23S	51.54E
20	45.18S	76.03E		21	48.12S	56.52E
21	45.26S	81.07E		22	47.51S	62.10E
22	45.53S	86.25E		23	47.44S	67.1 E
23	46.32S	91.52E		24	47.59S	72.33E
24	47.05S	96.30E		25	47.36S	79.24E
25	47.17S	102.44E		26	48.7 S	86.40E
26	47.04S	108.58E		27	48.33S	94.41E
27	46.23S	115.04E		28	48.28S	100.54E
28	45.29S	120.47E		29	49.16S	106.31E
29	44.45S	125.43E		30	49.33S	113.50E
30	44.04S	128.13E		31	49.57S	119.43E
31	43.25S	130.21E		1 November	50.18S	126.34E
1 November	42.50S	134.39E		2	49.7 S	134.2 E
2	42.03S	139.44E		3	48.24S	143.25E
3	41.08S	143.31E		4	45.48S	147.26E
4	39.56S	145.26E		5	43.6 S	149.46E
5	37.35S	149.55E		6	39.40S	151.22E
6	35.18S	150.37E		7	35.47S	151.23E
7	33.50S	151.18E		8	33.51S	151.11E

Finishing line – small hours

5 Finishing Times

LEG 1: LONDON–SYDNEY
Starting time was 31 August 1975, 10.20.00 G.M.T. (09.20 British Summer Time)

Great Britain II	6 November 1975 15.39.49 G.M.T.
Kriter II	6 November 1975 22.07.48 G.M.T.
CS e RB II	1 December 1975 16.26.50 G.M.T.
Great Escape	10 December 1975 23.10 G.M.T

LEG 2: SYDNEY–DOVER
**Starting time was 21 December 1975, 01.00.00 G.M.T.
(12.00 Eastern Australia Time)**

Great Britain II	25 February 1976 23.31.35 G.M.T.
Anaconda II	8 March 1976 23.07.45 G.M.T
Kriter II	25 March 1976 10.20.27 G.M.T
Great Escape	25 March 1976 20.48.40 G.M.T.
CS e RB II	5 April 1976 22.59.47 G.M.T.

Leg One London–Sydney, distance 13,650 miles.
Start Off Garrison Point at the confluence of the rivers Medway and Thames, on Sunday 31 August 1975 at 10.20 hours G.M.T.
Finish Sydney Heads – record by *Patriarch* in 1869/70 – 69 days.

Arrival Position	Yacht	Arrival Time	Elapsed Time days hrs. mins. secs.				Miles per day average	Time Allowance days hrs. mins. secs.				Corrected Time days hrs. mins. secs.				Place
1	Great Britain II	6 November – 15.39 G.M.T.	67	05	19	00	202.9	Scratch				67	05	19	00	2nd
2	Kriter II	6 November – 22.07 G.M.T	67	11	47	00	202.2	01	11	30	09	66	00	16	51	1st
3	CS e RB II	30 November – 18.30 G.M.T	91	08	10	00	149.5	12	18	21	38	77	13	48	22	3rd
4	The Great Escape	10 December – 12.30 G.M.T	101	02	10	00	135.0	14	01	24	16	87	00	45	44	4th

Leg Two Sydney–London, distance 12,730 miles.
Start Sydney Heads on Sunday 21 December 1975 at 0100 hours G.M.T.
Finish Off the Admiralty Pier lighthouse at Dover Harbour – record by *Patriarch* – 69 days.

Arrival Position	Yacht	Arrival Time	Elapsed Time				Miles per day average	Time Allowance				Corrected Time				Place
			days	hrs.	mins.	secs.		days	hrs.	mins.	secs.	days	hrs.	mins.	secs.	
1	*Great Britain II*	25 February – 23.31 G.M.T	66	22	31	35	192.8	Scratch				66	22	31	35	1st
2	*Anaconda II*	8 March – 2307 G.M.T	78	22	07	45	163.2	01	17	33	11	77	04	34	34	2nd
3	*Kriter II*	25 March – 10.20 G.M.T.	94	09	20	27	134.9	01	09	06	35	93	00	13	52	4th
4	*The Great Escape*	25 March – 20.48 G.M.T	94	19	48	40	134.3	13	02	39	48	81	17	08	52	3rd
5	*CS e RB II**	5 April – 22.59 G.M.T.	105	21	59	47	120.0	11	21	42	44	112	19	32	27	5th

Note
Kriter II (passage time from 17.1.76 at 00.04.18 G.M.T.)

		Arrival Time	days	hrs.	mins.	secs.	Miles per day average	days	hrs.	mins.	secs.	days	hrs.	mins.	secs.	
		25 March – 10.20 G.M.T.	68	10	16	09	185.0	01	09	06	35	67	01	09	34	

* Corrected Time increased by 20% – no independent generator on board, and failure to comply with reporting rules.

6 Prizes

Patriarch model

Model of the clipper that set the record passage times between England and Sydney and Sydney and England in 1869–70. Presented by the *Financial Times* as the first prize to the yacht with the shortest aggregate time over the two legs of the race.

Winner: *Great Britain II*.

The Cutty Sark *Silver Salver*

Presented by the Cutty Sark Society to the yacht second overall on elapsed time for the whole race.

Winner: *Kriter II*.

LEG 1: LONDON TO SYDNEY

The Silver Dolphin Trophy

Presented by the *Financial Times* to the yacht making the fastest passage on Leg 1.

Winner: *Great Britain II*, skipper Mike Gill.

Silver Salver

Presented by the Lord Mayor of Sydney to the second yacht on Leg 1.

Winner: *Kriter II*.

The Royal Ocean Racing Club Clock

Presented to the yacht with the best handicap passage time on Leg 1.

Winner: *Kriter II* (she beat *Great Britain II* on handicap by 29 hours 2 minutes 10 seconds).

LEG 2: SYDNEY TO DOVER

The Silver Albatross Trophy

Presented by the *Financial Times* to the yacht making the fastest passage on Leg 2.

Winner: *Great Britain II*, skipper Roy Mullender.

The Royal Ocean Racing Club Clock

Presented to the yacht with the best handicap passage time on Leg 2.

Winner: *Great Britain II*, skipper Roy Mullender.

The 'Australian' Trophy

Presented by News Limited of Australia to the second yacht on Leg 2.

Winner: *Anaconda II*.

The Punch Coronation Trophy

Presented by Melbourne Hart & Company Limited to the first yacht to cross the latitude line of Havana, Cuba, on Leg 2.

Winner: *Great Britain II*, skipper Roy Mullender.

7 Glossary

Aback:	the wind striking the back of the sail.
Abaft:	behind the line drawn through the centre of the boat amidships.
Abeam:	at 90 degrees to the yacht.
About:	when the direction of the relative wind is changed from one side of the yacht to the other. *See Tack.*
Aft:	behind.
Aground:	touching the sea bed.
Aloft:	on the mast or in the rigging.
Anticyclone:	an area of barometrical high pressure.
Antifouling:	a paint applied to the bottom of a yacht to prevent marine growth.
Apparent wind:	the wind as it is felt aboard the yacht, which need not be the wind actually blowing.
Back:	to pull a sail to windward to swing yacht. A wind which backs changes direction anticlockwise round the compass.
Backstay:	wire or wires from the top of any mast to the aft end of the yacht.
Batten:	wood or glassfibre stiffening in leach of sail.
Beacon:	radio transmitter in known position used to fix position of yacht in conjunction with other beacons or other fixing methods.
Beam ends:	the ends of deck cross beams. The side of yacht at deck level.
Bear away:	to turn away and run from direction of wind.
Beat:	to sail in direction, or as close as possible to, the direction of the wind.
Below:	beneath the deck.
Bilges:	the lowest part inside the hull.
Boom:	horizontal spar at the foot of sail, one end attached to a mast.
Broach:	lose control of yacht when running, and swing up towards wind, often with spars and sails downwind in the water.

Broad reach:	sailing with wind on the beam, or just aft of it with sails free.
Bulkhead:	main wall across the hull of yacht.
By the lee:	sailing down wind with sails set to the wrong side; often occurs accidentally when running dead before wind.
Clew:	corner of spinnaker or aft corner of mainsail, headsail, staysail or mizzen.
Close-hauled:	sailing hard on the wind, sails pinned in tight.
Cross sea:	a sea running at ninety degrees to the swell.
Cutter-rigged:	carrying two headsails, one astern of the other on a single-masted yacht, but applied to ketches when not carrying mizzen sail on aft mast.
Dead reckoning:	calculating yacht's progress by measurement of known speed, direction and speed of tide or current.
Deckhead:	ceiling in cabin.
Decklog:	navigational book kept by watch on deck and/or navigator to assess progress and position.
Depression:	cyclone. Low area of barometric pressure.
Deviation:	known error in compass.
Direction finding:	calculating position by radio bearings on beacons.
Draft (draught):	minimum depth of water needed to float the yacht.
Ebb:	falling of tide.
Echo sounder:	electronic measurer of depth.
Equinox:	time of equal daylight and darkness.
Fetch:	able to lay course without tacking.
Forestay:	wire rigged from bow to masthead. An inner forestay is rigged from aft of the bow to a lower point on the mast.
Free:	sailing with sails eased.
Front:	meteorological term for line between two air masses of different temperature.
Genoa:	a jib or headsail that overlaps the mainsail. Yachts in the Clipper Race carried genoas of varying sizes to meet different strength of wind, the largest, for the lighter wind strength, being number 1.
Go about:	tack.
Guardrail:	safety rail around the deck of a yacht, set at a regulation height.

Gybe:	bringing the wind from one quarter to the other when sailing off wind.
Halyard:	wire or rope for hoisting sails.
Headboard:	metal plate sewn into the top corner of a sail.
Headsail:	any sail set forward of the main mast.
Impeller:	small propeller set through the hull of the yacht below the waterline that sends impulses to a speed- or distance-measuring instrument.
I.O.R.:	the International Offshore Rule. Devised to produce a standard worldwide handicap enabling yachts of different sizes to race against one another.
Jib:	a headsail that does not overlap the mainsail.
Jury rig:	temporary rigging or steering gear put together in an emergency. *Kriter* rigged a jury rudder to return to Sydney.
Ketch:	yacht with two masts, the after one smaller and stepped forward of the rudder. This rig was used by all competing yachts except *CS e RB II*.
Knockdown:	capsize by the sea.
Latitude:	distance north or south of equator measured in degrees from the centre of the earth.
Lifeline:	line attached to safety harness worn by crew.
Longitude:	distance in degrees either east or west of Greenwich meridian.
Mizzen:	aft mast of a ketch or yawl, or the sail set on this mast.
Point:	to sail on the wind.
Pulpit:	metal frame on the bow of yacht to which guardrails are attached. A working support for crew on foredeck.
Rating:	the handicap formula arrived at for each yacht by the International Offshore Rule.
Reach:	sail with sails free and the wind abeam.
Rhumb line:	straight line drawn on Mercator chart.
Rudder stock:	the part of the rudder attached to stern of yacht's keel.
Run:	to sail with wind right aft.
Run:	distance covered during known period of time.
Scantlings:	measurement of the main frames and stringers in a yacht's hull.
Schooner:	two-masted sailing boat with main mast taller than the foremast, e.g. *CS e RB II*.

(To) sheet:	take in ropes controlling the position of the sails.
Shroud:	wire rigging supporting the mast on either side.
Sounding:	measurement of depth in 100 fathoms (600 feet) or less.
Spreader:	transverse support strut on mast.
Stanchion:	vertical post supporting guardrail.
Standing rigging:	shrouds and other fixed rigging supporting a mast.
Stay:	standing rigging in the fore and aft line. Backstay, forestay, inner forestay, for example.
Staysail:	sail hoisted inside main headsail, or from mizzen mast forward (mizzen staysail).
Tack:	sail to windward in stages, altering course to put wind from one side of the bow to the other.
Track:	course made good by yacht but not necessarily the course steered.
Trysail:	storm sail rigged in place of mainsail in extreme winds.
Transit:	in navigation, a line drawn with two or more known objects in line.
Winch:	mechanical crew-driven drum for hoisting sails or sheeting sails home. One form is the 'coffeegrinder' when one drum has two pairs of handles geared so two crew can winch together. A self-tailing winch has the ropes, or, more usually, the wire permanently attached to the drum.

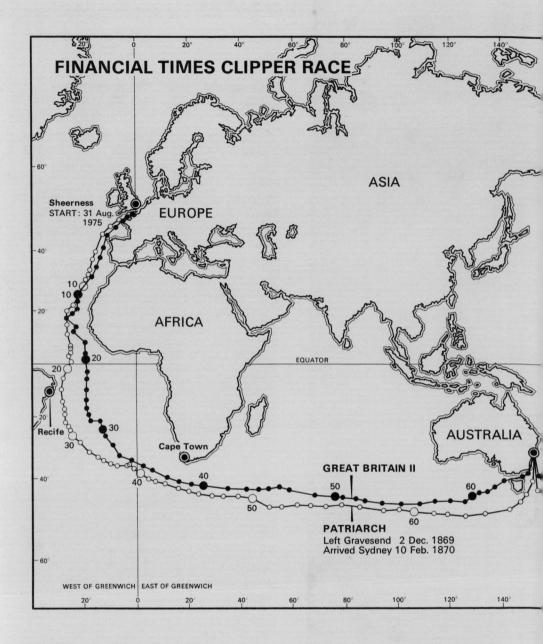

FINANCIAL TIMES CLIPPER RACE

Sheerness
START: 31 Aug.
1975

EUROPE

ASIA

AFRICA

EQUATOR

Recife

Cape Town

AUSTRALIA

GREAT BRITAIN II

PATRIARCH
Left Gravesend   2 Dec. 1869
Arrived Sydney 10 Feb. 1870

WEST OF GREENWICH | EAST OF GREENWICH